HAM HOUSE

Surrey

THE NATIONAL TRUST

Ham is on the south bank of the Thames, west of the A307 at Petersham. Richmond station (British Rail and London Underground) is $1\frac{1}{2}$ miles by footpath.

Acknowledgements

Chapter One has been written by Christopher Rowell; Chapter Two by Cathal Moore; and the Introduction and Chapters Three–Five by Nino Strachey, who also compiled the picture entries and the family tree. The National Trust has been fortunate to inherit the Victoria & Albert Museum's voluminous research archive on Ham, and is indebted to the museum's present and former staff for their expert advice and assistance. In pursuing further research, the Trust is grateful to the Tollemache family, and in particular to Lord Tollemache, Sir Lyonel Tollemache, Bt, the Hon. Michael Tollemache and Mr and Mrs Grant of Rothiemurchus, for allowing access to material in their possession, and for agreeing to its reproduction in this new guidebook. Chapter Two has drawn on David Mees's historical research into the garden, and Lesley Howes's archaeological investigations. The Trust is also indebted to Jennifer Kaner, who provided valuable information on the Vavasour family.

Photographs: Country Life Picture Library p. 27, 39, 76; National Trust pp. 11, 41; National Trust Photographic Library p. 78; NTPL/ Bill Batten pp. 1, 10, 28, 31, 32, 34, 36, 43, 62, 66, 68, 69; NTPL/Vera Collingwood p. 7; NTPL/Angelo Hornak p. 54; NTPL/Nick Meers pp. 4, 9; NTPL/Stephen Robson p. 57; NTPL/Rupert Truman pp. 21, 23, 42, 63, 67; John Paul Photography front cover, pp. 13, 15, 19, 22, 26, 33, 73; British Architectural Library, RIBA, London pp. 53, 55; The Lord Tollemache/Courtauld Institute of Art p. 71; The Hon. Michael Tollemache/Prudence Cuming p. 56; Victoria & Albert Museum Picture Library pp. 17, 40, 45, 50, 59, 60, 61, 65, 70, 72, 75, back cover.

First published in Great Britain in 1995 by the National Trust
© 1995 The National Trust
Registered charity no. 205846

ISBN 0 7078 0275 X

Designed by James Shurmer

Phototypeset in Monotype Bembo Series 270
by Southern Positives and Negatives (SPAN), Lingfield, Surrey (9805)

Printed in Great Britain by Balding + Mansell
for National Trust Enterprises Ltd,
36 Queen Anne's Gate, London SW1H 9AS

CONTENTS

Introduction   *page* 5

Chapter One Tour of the House   6

Plans of the House   8

Chapter Two Tour of the Garden   52

Chapter Three The 1st Earl and Countess of Dysart   60

Chapter Four The Duke and Duchess of Lauderdale   64

Chapter Five After 1698   70

Family Tree   77

Bibliography   78

Index   79

INTRODUCTION

Ham House was built in 1610 for Sir Thomas Vavasour, Knight Marshal to James I. On Sir Thomas's death in 1620, the house passed briefly to the Earl of Holdernesse, before becoming the home of William Murray in 1626. Murray was a childhood friend of Charles I, and a fellow connoisseur and collector. Between 1637 and 1639 he remodelled the interior of Ham, creating the Great Staircase and a suite of sumptuous rooms on the first floor: the Great Dining Room (now the Hall Gallery), the North Drawing Room, and the Long Gallery with its adjoining picture closet. When the Civil War broke out in 1642, Murray naturally joined the Royalist cause, and was created 1st Earl of Dysart in 1643. He spent the rest of his life in exile, making only brief visits to England, before dying in Edinburgh in 1655.

Having no male heir, Murray's title and property passed to his eldest daughter, Elizabeth, who was described as 'a woman of beauty', widely read and articulate, but 'restless in her ambition, profuse in her expense, and of a most ravenous covetousness'. Her first marriage was to Sir Lionel Tollemache, 3rd Bt, of Helmingham Hall in Suffolk, a wealthy and cultivated squire. Even before his death in 1669, Lady Dysart was rumoured to have formed an attachment to the ambitious John Maitland, 1st Duke of Lauderdale, Secretary of State for Scotland. Following their marriage in 1672, they extended and refurnished Ham as the palatial villa of one of the most powerful ministers of Charles II. Much of this luxurious interior decoration survives, together with pictures, furniture and textiles.

After the Duke's death in 1682, the Duchess had to curb her extravagance and was eventually reduced to pawning her favourite pictures and jewellery. Crippled by gout, and embittered by years of

legal wrangling with the Duke's relatives, Elizabeth died at Ham in 1698. Ham House and the Dysart title then passed to her eldest son from her first marriage: Lionel Tollemache, 3rd Earl of Dysart. Lionel had inherited the Tollemache estates nearly 30 years before, and took little interest in the house that had been so much his mother's creation.

By contrast, the 3rd Earl's grandson and heir, another Lionel, chose to make Ham a main family seat after his inheritance in 1727. The 4th Earl carried out major structural repairs (which included the rebuilding of the bays on the north and south fronts), and filled many of the rooms with new furniture and paintings. Most notably, the Queen's Bedchamber, built by the Lauderdales, was converted into a first-floor drawing-room, with the mahogany chairs, gilt mirrors and pier-tables, and tapestries after Watteau which survive in the room.

The 5th Earl was renowned for his rigid economy, and his only changes at Ham appear to have been a partial landscaping of the garden. He was succeeded in 1799 by his brother, Wilbraham, who immediately began a programme of improvements inside and outside the house. The 6th Earl was a generous patron of Reynolds and Gainsborough, and created the striking Yellow Satin Bedroom, but most of his changes were antiquarian in spirit, enhancing Ham's seventeenth-century character.

Little changed at Ham between the 6th Earl's death in 1821 and 1884, when William, 9th Earl of Dysart, came of age. Sixty years of benign neglect had left the house and its contents in urgent need of repair, and Lord Dysart embarked on a thorough restoration campaign: the roof was renewed, electricity and heating installed, and much of the seventeenth-century furniture repaired. The 9th Earl died in 1935, when Ham passed to his second cousin, Sir Lyonel Tollemache. Sir Lyonel and his son, Cecil, gave Ham to the National Trust in 1948.

(Opposite) The north front

CHAPTER ONE

TOUR OF THE HOUSE

The Exterior

THE NORTH FORECOURT

The stone piers and iron gate facing the river at the entrance to the Forecourt were designed by Sir William Bruce (c.1630–1710), a cousin of the Countess of Dysart, and erected in 1671. The stone was shipped from Longannet Quarry on the Firth of Forth. The painters' accounts (1673–4) record that the gates were painted blue and partly gilded (a scheme recently renewed). The Coade stone pineapples to either side were set up by the 6th Earl soon after his succession in 1799. The present railings were introduced by the 9th Earl in the early twentieth century.

Originally, the gateway and Forecourt were enclosed by walls, into which '38 heads of lead' were set, according to the 1679 inventory. Twenty-two of these remain in their original niches (finished in 1674), but the 6th Earl, having demolished the outer wall of the Forecourt, placed the remainder in niches on the façade of the house (an Italianate, Neoclassical and typically antiquarian arrangement entirely in keeping with John Evelyn's 1678 description of Ham as 'inferior to few Villas in Italy itself'). The busts include portraits of Charles I and Charles II (both great benefactors of the family), of Roman Emperors, and copies after the Antique. The three marble heads (in the arcades, or 'Cloisters' [see below], and above the central door) were possibly moved from the Great Staircase. As a centrepiece, the 6th Earl purchased the Coade stone *River God*, cast, like the bronze at Somerset House, London, from a model by John Bacon the Elder (1740–99).

Originally, instead of the circular carriage drive, a straight path (the width of the terrace steps) ran from the front door to the river flanked by a pair of statues on stone plinths, set up in 1673, and 'flower pots', mended in 1672. The 'Two carv'd wainscot benches' made 'for ye Garding [garden]'

by Henry Harlow in 1674 still stand in the 'Cloisters'. The clipped drums of bay, the box hedges and topiary with clipped Portugal laurels recall the planting that was here at the end of the nineteenth century.

THE NORTH FRONT

An unknown architect built Ham House in 1610, of red brick with stone dressings on the traditional H-plan. The projecting bays incorporating 'Cloisters' between the wings were originally surmounted by turrets with ogee caps. The alterations and extensions for the Duke and Duchess of Lauderdale may have been designed by Bruce, later Surveyor General of the King's Works in Scotland, and were executed in 1672–4 under the direction of another gentleman-architect, William Samwell, who certificated all the tradesmen's bills. The works entailed reducing the height of the turrets to give an even roof line, and filling in the space between the wings of the south front with a suite of rooms on each floor, as well as the renovation of the main house and its outbuildings.

By 1730 a detailed survey by the 4th Earl's architect, John James, revealed serious structural problems, and extensive repairs were undertaken (largely between 1742 and 1747). However, the seventeenth-century elevations were preserved and most of the bay-windows were rebuilt.

FRONTISPIECE

One considerable alteration was made on the north front in the 1740s: the projecting frontispiece above the stone front doorcase had 'drawn off from the Wall, from the bottom to the top' and had 'gone so far as to endanger even pulling the Roof after it'. The doorcase was preserved, but the frontispiece with its bay-windows was removed. The doorcase is probably contemporary with the front door (dated 1610 and bearing the loyal inscription 'Vivat

Rex'), which was 'graind' by the Duke's painter in 1673–4 (decoration that has recently been renewed).

The arms painted above are (on the left) the horse's head crest of the Tollemache family surmounted by an earl's coronet and (on the right) Tollemache (*Quarterly 1 and 4 argent, a fret sable*) quartering Dysart, in commemoration of the marriage in 1648 between Elizabeth, Countess of Dysart and Sir Lionel Tollemache.

THE EAST FRONT

This still retains much of its seventeenth-century fenestration. The elaborate doorcase in the centre gives access to the Great Staircase, and the glazed door to the left allowed the Duchess of Lauderdale to enter the Cherry Garden from her private apartment, constructed in 1672–4.

THE SOUTH FRONT

The centre of the 1610 house was set back from the projecting wings in accordance with the traditional Jacobean H-plan. This was filled in by the Lauderdales between 1672 and 1674 to provide a series of rooms facing south over the garden, with access to it via a double-flight staircase from the central Marble Dining Room. The earlier mullioned and transomed stone windows and bay-windows were preserved from the wings of the 1610 house, but otherwise the new windows were provided with sashes, made to resemble the older fenestration. The extent of the Lauderdales' alterations can be seen in several images, the earliest *c.*1671, the latest being published by Colen Campbell in 1739. This confirms the evidence of the documents: that the 4th Earl's alterations were mainly of the 1740s, despite the fact that he commissioned a survey of the building in 1730, which informed him that the bay-

The Coade stone river god on the North Forecourt

PLANS OF THE HOUSE

1 The Great Hall
2 The Chapel
3 The Great Staircase
17 The Marble Dining Room
18 The Withdrawing Room
19 The Volury Room
20 The White Closet
21 The Duchess's Private Closet
22 The Duke's Dressing Room
23 The Duchess's Bedchamber
24 The Duke's Closet
25 The Steward's Hall
26 The Back Parlour

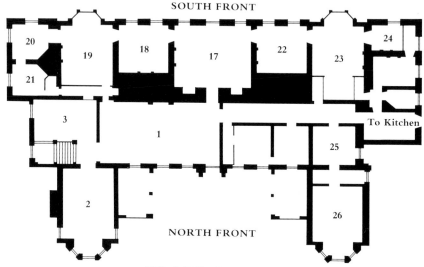

GROUND FLOOR

4 The Yellow Satin Bedroom (*closed*)
5 The Yellow Satin Dressing Room (*closed*)
6 The Museum Room
7 The Chapel Chamber Closet (*closed*)
8 The Hall Gallery
9 The North Drawing Room
10 The Long Gallery
11 The Green Closet
12 The Library Closet
13 The Library
14 The Antechamber to the Queen's Bedchamber
15 The Queen's Bedchamber
16 The Queen's Closet

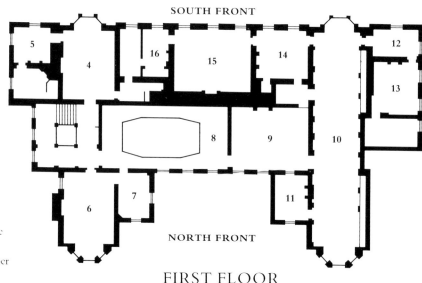

FIRST FLOOR

The south front

windows were 'entirely ruinous and incapable of Repair otherwise than by rebuilding them, and the sooner this is done the better'. This he did, but replaced the third tier with Venetian windows fronted by balustrades. He also removed the hipped roofs above, reducing the roof-line to cornice level. All the windows were given sashes of the familiar type, apart from the horizontal ovals lighting the Basement, which survive unchanged from the Lauderdale period.

THE WEST SIDE

Seventeenth-century mullions and transoms can be seen on the left; to the right are mid-eighteenth-century sashes. This has always been the service entrance. The principal door gives on to the West Passage, while to the left, steps lead down to the basement. Outside, as now, there was a yard around which, or nearby, were grouped such buildings as the bake-house, still-house, wash-house, bath-house and brew-house. There was also a dairy, which may have always been where it is today – on one side of the courtyard gate. In 1683 the Dairy contained all the tools of the milkmaid's craft including milking pails, pans, 'skimming dishes' and a 'Strayner'. There were 'Eight China dishes' and a 'white Sillabub pot', as well as cheese-making equipment: a 'Cheese tubb' and 'Cheese presse'.

The Dairy was given its present fittings in the late eighteenth century or early nineteenth century. The legs of the side-tables (in the form of cow's legs, with bovine heads as capitals) and the decorative tiles are more evocative of the world of Marie Antoinette than that of the more functional seventeenth-century dairy. However, the occasional visits of the family and their guests (once visits to the Dairy had become a fashionable entertainment), would not have unduly impeded the serious work of making butter and cheese. (*The Dairy is not, at present, open.*)

The Interior

An asterisk denotes a picture listed in the 1683 'Estimate of Pictures'.

THE GREAT HALL AND HALL GALLERY

Part of the 1610 building, the then single-storey Great Hall contained by 1655 ' A Long shovel-board table' (for a game like shove-halfpenny) and a 'draw table', which suggests that the room was occasionally used for dining. By 1677–83 it was hung with weaponry, of a martial and sporting character, and 'Two drums wt. sticks', an echo of the days when entrance halls served as guard rooms. By 1677 shuffle board had given way to billiards,

The Great Hall

the billiard-table having 'balls of Ivory' and 'two clubbs tipt. with Ivory'. The room immediately above was 'the Great Dining Roome'.

The original panelling (subsequently altered) was painted in 1638 in imitation of walnut. The black and white marble floor is probably part of the original construction of the room. The dais, at the east end, has been relaid using the original seventeenth-century parquet (previously in store) with additions.

The ceiling was pierced *c.*1698–1728 to create the present hall and first-floor gallery. The stone-colour scheme, recently re-created, was first applied *c.*1770. Previously, the Great Hall appears to have been painted grey, the Hall Gallery various shades of green (or covered, after *c.*1735, with a turquoise wallpaper).

CHIMNEYPIECE

The ormolu mounts and the plaster figures of *Mars* and *Minerva*, *c.*1640, have been attributed to Francesco Fanelli (active *c.*1609–*c.*1665), a Florentine who came to England in the early 1630s and who worked for Charles I and his court. The family tradition that the plaster statues represent William Murray, 1st Earl of Dysart and his Countess, Katherine Bruce, should not be entirely dismissed. The female figure bears some resemblance to the gilt bronze bust of Lady Dysart in the White Closet, attributed to Hubert Le Sueur (*c.*1585–1658), a French sculptor working for the Crown (see p.41). The figures may be in masque costume, and they hold the crests of Murray (a mermaid) and of Bruce (a tree issuing from an earl's coronet). An alternative attribution to Le Sueur should, perhaps, be considered. However, the figure of *Minerva* is also closely comparable to a *Minerva* by Jérôme Duquesnoy the Younger (d.1654) on the Grand Staircase of the Residenz at Regensburg in Bavaria.

PICTURES

The pictures in the Great Hall have been hung in their 1844 order, which explains the rather curious jamming together of the portraits of the 4th Earl and Countess of Dysart at the dais end.

NORTH (WINDOW) WALL:

ENGLISH, *c.*1777
Captain John Tollemache, RN (1744–77)
Third son of the 4th Earl of Dysart, tragically killed in a duel at sea. When his only son, Lionel Robert, died at the siege of Valenciennes in 1793, the hope of any continuation of the Dysart male line came to an end. The 5th and 6th Earls died childless, and the title passed to their surviving sister, Lady Louisa Manners. Probably a posthumous portrait done from a miniature.

Manner of PIETER POURBUS the Elder (1523–84)
Portrait of an Old Man
A Flemish picture, wrongly inscribed as Sir Lionel Tollemache, 1st Bt (1562?–1621), by 'Frederico Zaccaro'.

Sir GODFREY KNELLER, Bt (1646/9–1723)
Henrietta Cavendish, Lady Huntingtower (d.1717/18)

Illegitimate daughter of the 2nd Duke of Devonshire and his mistress, Mrs Heneage (see her portrait in the Hall Gallery). Married in 1706 to Lionel, Lord Huntingtower, eldest son of the 3rd Earl of Dysart. Dressed in riding habit and painted *c.*1715.

EAST (STAIRCASE) WALL:

JOHN VANDERBANK (1694?–1739)
Lionel Tollemache, 4th Earl of Dysart (1708–70)
Lionel inherited Ham and the Tollemache estates on the death of his grandfather, the 3rd Earl, in 1727. On his return from the Grand Tour in 1728 he began extensive refurbishments at both Ham and Helmingham Hall in Suffolk, which continued until the 1750s. Shown in peer's robes.

JOHN VANDERBANK (1694?–1739)
Lady Grace Carteret, Countess of Dysart (1713–55)
Signed: *J.ᵗ Vanderbank Fecit 1737*
Eldest daughter of John, 2nd Baron Carteret and 2nd Earl Granville (see his portrait in the Library Closet). She married the 4th Earl of Dysart in 1729, and was a talented amateur artist, painting pastel portraits of her family, and decorating furniture with elaborate shellwork.

The Great Hall in 1904

SOUTH (FIREPLACE) WALL:

After Sir ANTHONY VAN DYCK (1599–1641)
James Stuart, 4th Duke of Lennox and 1st Duke of Richmond (1612–55)
A close relative of Charles I and an ardent Royalist during the Civil War. Although Stuart was a contemporary of William Murray, this portrait is not listed at Ham before 1770. The original, of *c.*1633, is in the Metropolitan Museum, New York.

OVER FIREPLACE:

ITALIAN, early seventeenth-century
Landscape with the Good Samaritan
Recorded here in the 1655 inventory.

After Sir ANTHONY VAN DYCK (1599–1641)
Lady Honora de Burgh, Marchioness of Winchester (1610/11–61/2)
Daughter of the Earl of Clanricarde and St Albans, and second wife of John, 5th Marquess of Winchester, who defended Basing House near Basingstoke as a Royalist stronghold until 1645.

WEST WALL:

Sir JOSHUA REYNOLDS, PRA (1723–92)
Charlotte Walpole, Countess of Dysart (1738–89)
Inscribed with the sitter's and artist's names, and dated 1775
The illegitimate daughter of Sir Edward Walpole, granddaughter of Sir Robert Walpole and niece of Horace Walpole. She married the 5th Earl of Dysart in 1760.

JOHN HOPPNER, RA (1758–1810) after Sir JOSHUA REYNOLDS, PRA (1723–92)
Lady Louisa Manners, 7th Countess of Dysart (1745–1840)
The eldest daughter of the 4th Earl of Dysart, and sister of the 5th and the 6th Earl, whom she succeeded as Countess in her own right in 1821. The original (painted in 1779) is in the Iveagh Bequest, Kenwood.

FURNITURE

The Hall chairs, of oak, the splats painted with the Tollemache arms and an earl's coronet, were supplied to the 4th Earl by George Nix, a London cabinetmaker who was paid £18 in 1730 'for 18 Hall Chairs Painted and Varnisht'. Nix received £430 13s 6d for his work at Ham between 1729 and 1734.

*The pair of mahogany side-tables with green marble tops, c.*1730, is from a set of three (the third is in the Inner Hall). The wrought-iron radiator cover on the east wall displaced one of these tables in the late nineteenth century; the other (beneath the windows) is a copy (1993).

THE CHAPEL

Until the 1670s this was the family's principal living-room, furnished both for relaxation and for dining. The 1655 inventory reveals that the décor (of *c.*1640, and therefore contemporary with the 1st Earl's new staircase and upstairs State Apartment) was a unified scheme based on red and gold. The walls were hung with red and gold leather, which also bordered the scarlet curtains, upholstery and even the table-carpets. The curtains at the bay windows (hidden by the altar) were 'divided' (ie there were two which pulled together, instead of a single curtain), something that we now take for granted, but which was then a novelty, originating from Paris.

From 1672 the room became a chapel, the last item of joinery being supplied in December 1674. The black and white marble floor of the altar dais was laid in 1674 by the mason John Lampen. The richness of its 'Crimsin Velvett and Damask' hangings and the comfort of its 'Eighteen Hassuks' (kneelers) and 'Cusheones of Damask', as described in 1677, may seem strange given the simplicity prescribed by the Duke of Lauderdale's Presbyterian faith. However, in later life he turned against the Scottish Presbyterians, and the rich furnishings of the Chapel reveal a distaste for the asceticism of their places of worship. On the Duke's death in 1682, the crimson hangings were put into store, and were replaced by mourning weeds of 'black velvet', which were still in place when the 1683 inventory was taken.

FURNITURE

'*Their Grace's two pews*', box pews with doors, supplied with kneeling stools, are on either side of the entrance. This furniture, the lecterns and the remaining woodwork was supplied by the joiner Henry Harlow in 1673 and 1674.

The Chapel;
watercolour by
H. W. Brewer, 1886
(private collection)

TEXTILES

Of the original crimson furnishings, the embroidered altar-hangings, the richly appointed book cushions and the silk velvet covering the reading desks of the ducal pews all survive. The wall-hangings are nineteenth-century replacements of the original 'Crimson velvett and Damask', probably associated with the fitting-up of the Chapel for Roman Catholic services by the mother of the 9th Earl, Katherine Huntingtower, in the second half of the nineteenth century.

METALWORK

Lighting was provided by 'brasse Candlesticks', some of which are still *in situ*, and by 'Tenn Sconces of brasse hung with gould and Silke Strings with tassells'. The present set of silvered sconces is probably Dutch, late nineteenth-century, though in seventeenth-century style.

THE GREAT STAIRCASE

Constructed in 1638–9 for William Murray by the joiner Thomas Carter, the plasterer Joseph Kinsman, and the painter Matthew Goodricke, the Staircase was designed as a magnificent prelude to the splendours of the upstairs State Apartment. The balustrade (carved with trophies of war), the panelling and the window architraves were originally painted (like the panelling of the Great Hall) to resemble walnut, with the principal doorcases and the arch into the Great Hall painted in imitation of white 'polished marble'. Gilding was limited to the mouldings around the balustrade trophies, the ovals in the panelling of the Inner Hall and elements of the plaster window architraves and the doorcases.

When the staircase was redecorated and slightly remodelled *c.*1673–4, this discreet gilding was augmented in particular by extensive picking-out of the balustrade trophies in silver-leaf toned to resemble gold (a cheaper form of gilding). Paint analysis has failed to reveal the wall-colour that went with these two early schemes, as well as other elements of their decoration. For the time being, the staircase has, therefore, been redecorated according to its subsequent treatment by the Tollemache family. It was probably the 6th Earl in the nineteenth century who combined walnut graining of the balustrade and other woodwork, with picking out in bronze. This has been simulated exactly, with dark red walls and bronzing (as recorded in 1844) of the seven plaster busts after the Antique.

SCULPTURE

In 1677 there were '4 heads of plaster' and '4 Marble heads'; the latter may have been moved outside to ornament the façade by the 6th Earl. Previously painted to resemble marble, the present busts are placed over the doors and on three wooden brackets bearing the Lauderdale cipher. There were originally four brackets (made in 1673) set in recessed roundels (like the busts outside): 'holes in ye starecase for ye heads to stand in' were completed in 1672. That these recesses no longer exist suggests that the walls were replastered and certainly the treads and boards of the stairs were replaced, probably in the nineteenth century.

PICTURES

The sombre tones of the early nineteenth-century decorative scheme are in keeping with the darkened seventeenth-century paintings in contemporary carved frames. Only two were originally gilded (according to the Lauderdale inventories) and these were stripped when the frames were renovated, probably in the late nineteenth century. Most of the pictures have probably been here since 1639; they have been hung in the sequence recorded in 1844.

PICTURES (INNER HALL)

After ABRAHAM BLOEMAERT (1564–c.1651)
*The Angel appearing to the Shepherds**
Probably part of William Murray's collection, since it is in an early seventeenth-century frame, like other pictures on the stairs that seem to have belonged to him. It is one of many copies of an engraving for which Bloemaert supplied the design.

Attributed to CORNELIUS VROOM (1591–1661)
*The Battle of Lepanto**
The battle, between a Christian alliance and the Turks, took place on 7 October 1571. Probably painted c.1615–18, and likely to have been part of Murray's collection.

FURNITURE

The Hall chairs and the green marble-topped side-table (all c.1730) belong to sets already described in the Great Hall (see p.12).

PICTURES (GREAT STAIRCASE)

After CORREGGIO (c.1489–1534)
*The 'School of Love' (Mercury, Venus and Cupid)**
The original of c.1524 was in Charles I's collection, and is now in the National Gallery, London. The King probably allowed Murray to have this copy painted, or gave it to him, in the late 1630s, to decorate his new 'Great Stair'.

? MIGUEL DE LA CRUZ (active c.1630–60) after TITIAN (1488/90–1576)
*Venus and Adonis**
In 1623 Murray accompanied the future Charles I to Spain in his quest for a Spanish bride. There de la Cruz was commissioned by Charles to copy paintings in Philip IV's collection. De la Cruz later worked for Charles in England, and in the late 1630s Murray acquired a series of his copies for the new staircase. The original is in the Prado.

MIGUEL DE LA CRUZ (active c.1630–60) after TITIAN (1488/90–1576)
*Diana and Actaeon**
Another copy of a painting formerly in Philip IV's collection, which suggests that it was a gift from Charles I to Murray. The original is on loan to the National Gallery of Scotland.

DIRCK VAN DEN BERGEN (1640–95)
*Landscape with Cattle**
Signed on a chest on the cart: *DVB*
Van den Bergen worked at Ham in the 1670s, supplying inset paintings of similar subjects for the Duke and Duchess of Lauderdale. This is the most ambitious picture by him in the house.

MIGUEL DE LA CRUZ (active c.1630–60) after TITIAN (1488/90–1576)
*Venus and a Satyr – The 'Venus del Pardo'**
The original was given to Charles I by Philip IV in 1623, and is now in the Louvre. This copy was probably made for Charles to give to Murray.

JACOB DE GHEYN II (1565–1629)
*Julius Caesar writing and dictating to his Scribes**
Signed (with ligature): *JDGheijn fe*
Caesar was famous for being able to dictate to a number of secretaries simultaneously. Again, this

The Great Staircase; watercolour by H. W. Brewer (private collection)

may have been purchased by Murray for his new staircase. De Gheyn was in London with his son in 1622.

MIGUEL DE LA CRUZ (active *c*.1630–60) after
TITIAN (1488/90–1576)
*Venus and Organ Player**
Copied from a version of this subject in Philip IV's collection, now in the Prado.

ADRIAEN VAN NIEULANDT (1587–1658)
*Diana with Nymphs**
Signed: *Adriaen van Nieulandt Fecit A°. 1615*
Probably bought by Murray for this position.

THE YELLOW SATIN BEDROOM

(LADY MAYNARD'S CHAMBER)

The intention here is to re-create the 6th Earl's *c*.1813 décor of striped yellow silk wall-hangings combined with curtains and upholstery of eighteenth-century yellow silk trimmed with crimson. In view of the expense, the room will have to remain closed for the time being.

Always a richly appointed bedroom, and part of the original structure of the house, the room was hung by 1655 with landscape tapestries and provided with a 'french bedstead' upholstered in green embroidered cloth *en suite* with curtains and seat upholstery. By 1679, when it was known as 'My Lady Maynard's Chamber' (after the Duchess of Lauderdale's sister, Margaret), the tapestries were 'the history of Vulcan' and the bed and furniture were covered with 'purpure damask', replaced by 1683 with 'blew figured velvet'. The two little rooms adjoining (a dressing-room and servant's bedchamber) were served by back stairs.

The *c*.1920 photograph reveals the 6th Earl's 'French striped satin hangings . . . panelled with rich embroidered border and furnished with gold mouldings'. These can be re-created, but the conservation of the bed-hangings will be complicated.

THE MUSEUM ROOM

An important bedchamber, described as the 'Roome over ye Chappell' in 1679 and hung with tapestry both then and in 1655. Adjacent was a closet, also accessible from the Hall Gallery, which contained another bed and functional furniture including a chest-of-drawers and a close-stool. The room is now a museum of textiles where fragments and individual pieces of upholstered furniture are displayed in cases to inhibit their further deterioration.

THE HALL GALLERY

Until the floor was pierced, probably between 1698 and 1728, this was the Great Dining Room, the first room of the State Apartment created by the 1st Earl between *c*.1637 and 1639. The architect Inigo Jones was the leading exponent of the court style of Charles I, of which the Ham State Apartment is a rare survival. However, it is likely that Franz Cleyn (see p.18) was the designer and co-ordinator of the late 1630s interior decoration at Ham.

The coffered ceiling, of Italianate inspiration, is by Kinsman, the plasterer, and has always been painted white, without gilding. The fireplace was in the centre of the wall opposite the windows. In 1638–9 the cornice, doorcases and dado were painted by Matthew Goodricke 'fair blew in Oylle . . . having all the Inrichments and Carving thereof guilt with fine gould'. According to the 1655 inventory, the walls were hung with 'tapestries of the storie of Phaeton'. Also listed were the two 'side-board tables' that may be the ones still in the Long Gallery (see p.24) and a dining-table. In store was a 'canopie of damask', which may have been used here to mark the seat of honour. By 1677 the upholstery of the chairs and the curtains had changed from yellow, blue and silver to crimson.

PICTURES

EAST WALL (INSET OVER DOOR):

Manner of FRANZ CLEYN (1582–1658)
Naked Boys with Lions
Before the opening up of the Great Dining Room floor, there were three 'Landskips' by Cleyn as overmantel and overdoors. For biography of Cleyn, see p.18.

EAST WALL:

CORNELIUS JONSON VAN CEULEN (1593–1661)
*William, 2nd Duke of Hamilton (1616–51), with John, Earl (later Duke) of Lauderdale (1616–82)**
Signed: *Cornelius Jonson v. C. fecit 1649*

Painted when these two Scottish peers were in exile in Holland with Charles II. Both returned to England to fight for the King at the Battle of Worcester (1651), where Hamilton was killed and Lauderdale captured.

SOUTH WALL:

Sir PETER LELY (1618–80) and Studio
Mrs Heneage
The mistress of the 2nd Duke of Devonshire and mother of Henrietta Cavendish, Lady Hunting-tower, whose portrait is in the Great Hall below. Lely's assistant may have been William Wissing (1655–87).

Sir PETER LELY (1618–80)
Elizabeth Murray, Countess of Dysart and Duchess of Lauderdale (1626–98)
A loyal supporter of Charles II, she risked her life during the Commonwealth as a member of the Sealed Knot, a group of Royalists who corresponded in code with the Court in exile. After the Restoration she was rewarded with a pension, and became a prominent member of the Carolean court. Following the death of her first husband, Sir Lionel Tollemache, in 1669, she resumed an old affair with the Earl (later Duke) of Lauderdale (see pendant nearby). They married in 1672 and then set about enlarging and redecorating Ham, which she had inherited from her mother in 1649.

Sir GODFREY KNELLER, Bt (1646/9–1723)
Lieutenant-General Thomas Tollemache (c.1651–94)
Second son of Elizabeth Murray and Sir Lionel Tollemache, and brother of the 3rd Earl of Dysart. He became a national hero after the Battle of Landau in 1693 and was killed a year later at the siege of Brest. Apparently enlarged by the artist from a head-and-shoulders, perhaps posthumously.

ENGLISH, c.1735
Lady Grace Carteret, Countess of Dysart (1713–55), with a child, black servant, and a cockatoo
She married the 4th Earl of Dysart in 1729. Painted c.1735, probably to celebrate the birth of a male heir, Lionel, the future 5th Earl (1734–99). She and the child are in 'Vandyck' dress. Black servants were considered a status symbol at that period.

? Sir GODFREY KNELLER, Bt (1646/9–1723)
Frances Worsley, Baroness Carteret (1694–1743)
The daughter of Sir Robert Worsley, 4th Bt, and the Hon. Frances Thynne, Lady Worsley, and

mother of Grace, Countess of Dysart. She married John, Baron Carteret, afterwards Earl Granville, in 1710. Possibly a later imitation by Vanderbank.

? After Sir PETER LELY (1618–80)
John Maitland, Duke of Lauderdale (1616–82)
One of Charles II's most powerful ministers, from 1661 to 1680 he was Secretary of State for Scotland, where he assumed almost vice-regal powers. Following the death of his first wife, Lady Anne Home, in 1671, he married Elizabeth Murray, Countess of Dysart (see pendant).

CHARLES JERVAS (1675–1739)
The Hon. Frances Thynne, Lady Worsley (1673–1750)
Only daughter of Thomas, 1st Viscount Weymouth, she married Sir Robert Worsley, 4th Bt, in 1690. The mother of Frances Worsley, Baroness Carteret, and grandmother of Grace Carteret, Countess of Dysart.

WEST WALL:

Sir PETER LELY (1618–80)
*The Duke and Duchess of Lauderdale**
Hung here by 1679, it represents the couple at the height of their power, when ministers, ambassadors

Wilbraham, 6th Earl of Dysart as a Boy (Hall Gallery)

and royalty were entertained at Ham. The rather dry pigment and free handling are characteristic of Lely's style in the last decade of his career.

WEST WALL (INSET OVER DOOR):

After ADAM ELSHEIMER (1578–1610)
*Tobias and the Angel**
Tobias, a Jew from Nineveh, is accompanied on his journey to Media to collect a debt for his father, Tobit, by the Archangel Raphael. The original is in the Historisches Museum, Frankfurt. Hung as a framed picture in 1683.

NORTH WALL:

ENGLISH, *c*.1750
Wilbraham, 6th Earl of Dysart (1739–1821) as a Boy
He inherited Ham from his elder brother in 1799, and immediately embarked upon a series of improvements inside and outside the house. He was a noted patron of Reynolds and Gainsborough, and created the striking Yellow Satin Bedroom, but the majority of his changes were antiquarian in spirit, enhancing Ham's existing seventeenth-century character. This is a very early representation of the instruments of shuttlecock and battledore.

FURNITURE

The mahogany armchairs, from two similar sets, *c*.1760, are of 'Windsor' type but without the usual upper part to the back. They are probably the 'Twelve low mahogany circular back chairs with cushions to ditto, covered with silk' listed in 1844.

THE NORTH DRAWING ROOM

This was the room to which guests withdrew from the Great Dining Room. The ceiling and frieze are by Kinsman, who was paid £35 4s, and the panelling and doorcases of French inspiration (on the window side) are by Carter, the joiner, all put up between 1637 and 1639. The marble chimneypiece with its distinctive surround of carved and gilded Solomonic columns is contemporary. The twisted columns with Ionic capitals derive from Raphael's cartoons of the *Acts of the Apostles* (Royal Collection, on loan to the V & A), which belonged to Charles I and served as models for the Mortlake tapestry works where Franz Cleyn, the probable

designer of this room and the painter of the inset pictures (see below), was director.

In 1655 the room was hung with five further tapestries from the 'storie of Phaeton' series in the Great Dining Room (now Hall Gallery). Despite the room's function as a post-prandial sitting-room, there was a 'large french bedstead' hung with 'white satine richly embroidered with needle work' matching the 'Two great chaires', the 'ten folding chaires', the curtains and even the carpet, creating an impressive and unified effect. Given the smaller size of Ham before the 1670s extensions, the room must have doubled as a State Bedroom, assuming the ceremonial function of the pre-seventeenth-century Great Chamber, in which a bed was customarily placed.

Probably painted white from the beginning, the 'wte Withdrawing Room' (as it was called in 1679) then no longer contained a bed, though it was still hung with the Phaeton tapestries (three rather than five). The doorway to the left of the fireplace was installed between 1679 and 1683 to communicate with the Queen's Bedchamber beyond.

PICTURES

FRANZ CLEYN (1582–1658)
Having made his name at the Danish Court, Cleyn arrived in England in 1625 at the invitation of James I. In *c*.1637–9 he supplied a series of inset paintings for the State Rooms at Ham redecorated by Murray. The pictures in this room seem to have been loosely inspired by the Polidoro paintings that served as models for those in the Green Closet, and are also in tempera on paper, as tapestry cartoons would have been.

INSET OVER EAST DOOR:

Three Putti playing with a Leopard

INSET OVER SOUTH DOOR:

Two Putti and a Satyr with bunches of grapes
This is a later introduction, out of scale with the others, and probably not by Cleyn.

INSET OVER FIREPLACE:

Two Putti offering a Baby a bunch of grapes
The baby is taken from one of Van Dyck's portraits of Charles I's children.

The North Drawing Room; watercolour by
H. W. Brewer, 1886 (private collection)

INSET OVER WEST DOOR:

Two Putti and a Goat

INSET OVER DOOR TO GREEN CLOSET:

After GUIDO RENI (1575–1642)
*Head of Helen**
Taken from Reni's *Rape of Helen,* now in the
Louvre. Hung as a framed picture in 1683.

FURNITURE

RANGED AGAINST WALLS:

The so-called 'Dolphin' chairs are part of a set of
twelve, six with arms and six without (one may be
seen with its upholstery uncovered in the Museum
Room, see p.16; all but one of those on open display

here are protected by case covers). This immensely
rare Parisian seat-furniture of *c.*1670–80 was originally gilded, silvered and painted in marine colours
to suggest dolphins sporting in their natural element. They were repainted and gilded, probably by
the 6th Earl, in the early nineteenth century. The
1677 inventory lists:

Six Arme chaires with carved and guilded frames
covered with Brocade with changeable cessnutt [sarse-
net: i.e. silk] cases [case-covers].
Six back stooles of ye same
[added later] white paragon cases for . . . chaires.

It is possible that the upholstery (a *brocatelle*) is
seventeenth-century, but it is more likely to be
nineteenth-century. In 1673 the Huguenot cabinetmaker and upholsterer Jean Poitevin, who worked
extensively for the English crown, was paid £6,
perhaps for upholstering these chairs in red.

    This French furniture is a reminder that the

Duchess of Lauderdale visited France on several occasions and that both she and her father looked to Paris as the main inspiration for their interiors. These chairs, and the other surviving French or French-inspired pieces at Ham (as well as the magnificent furniture described in bills and inventories), are a reflection of the pervading influence in northern Europe of the style of Louis XIV's court.

RIGHT OF FIREPLACE:

The ivory cabinet, first mentioned in the 1677 inventory, when it was provided with its own case-cover, was then an immensely expensive object (ivory being a rare commodity). Because of its value as a status symbol, it was moved to the Queen's Bedchamber between 1679 and 1683. It is likely to have been made *c*.1655–60 and is probably Flemish or Dutch, but it is possible that it was one of Lady Dysart's Parisian acquisitions.

FLANKING CABINET:

The carved and gilt candlestands are not mentioned in the 1670s and 1683 inventories, but their early date, *c*.1640, and the similarity to the chimneypiece of their twisted columns entwined with vines, suggest that they were part of the original décor.

The chandelier of gilded bronze may date from the 1670s, although the 1679 description does not quite fit: 'One hanging branch of brass blackt over'. However, it is probably the 1728 'Branch for Eight candles' and was certainly described in 1844 as 'An antique eight branch engraved bronze chandlier, with curiously wrought medallions on ditto'. It has undergone considerable restoration.

TEXTILES

By 1728 the 'Phaeton' tapestries hung here in the seventeenth century had been replaced by 'Damask hangings', which in 1844 were described as 'rich embroidered . . . (the colours quite gone)'. The latter wall-coverings were presumably put up between 1683 and 1698 by the Duchess of Lauderdale, as a watercolour of 1886 (illustrated on p.19) shows them to have been seventeenth-century. (A fragment is shown in the Museum Room.) The watercolour also indicates that the curtains were 'yellow satin with rich crimson border' – an eighteenth-century fabric once used in several rooms (a chair-cover in mint condition is in the Museum Room, see p.16).

The tapestries were hung here by 1911 and were woven for the 1st Lord Shelburne; the baron's coronet dates them between 1699 and 1719, when he was created an earl. Of silk and wool, they were probably woven in the London workshop of Stephen de May. The designs (part of a set of the *Months*) are based on cartoons for the Mortlake *Months* first woven for Charles, Prince of Wales, in 1623. They are hung in an arbitrary sequence, and in the case of *August* a panel from another set (after Teniers) has been inserted. Left wall: *Milking* (April); *Ploughing and Sowing* (September). Fireplace wall: *Sheep-shearing and Haymaking* (June and July). Right wall: *Hawking, Reaping* (May and August), *The Vintage* (October).

The carpet is Indian, *c*.1650. It is unclear how long this and its pair (in store) have been at Ham, but several extremely expensive carpets were bought by the Lauderdales both for the floor and for tables.

The single sun curtains were described in 1677 and 1679 as 'white damask fringd', and this material has been copied. By 1683 they were green and white with 'Sarsnet Shashes painted' (painted silk stretched on frames with the effect of transparencies) fitted into the window embrasures.

THE LONG GALLERY

The Long Gallery formed part of the original house, but was completely remodelled by William Murray in 1639. Carter, the joiner's, bill reads:

Item in the Gallerie wainscott that was taken asunder and new made and all the mouldings of the wainscot at 4s. the yarde £36.0.0.
Item for new work with the pedistalls 72 yards at 6s. the yarde £21.12.0.
Item 20 palasters [the Ionic pilasters] of my one [own] stuff £10.10.0.

The 1639 joinery, painted dark brown and partly gilded, remains intact, although there were alterations during the 1670s enlargement of Ham, notably the doorways at the far end into the new Library Closet and Queen's Antechamber. The panelling was 'Clensed & varnished' in 1673 and the gilding was renewed. The floor was also relaid; the present parquet floor is a further renewal, by the 9th Earl in the late nineteenth century. In 1677 the room was described as the 'Matted Gallery', which suggests woven rush matting, often made in Norfolk.

PICTURES

No pictures were listed here or elsewhere in the 1655 inventory, but it is likely that the Gallery was already hung with portraits. In 1679 there were 'Two and Twenty pictures' in the surviving 'carvd guilt frames', some of which were supplied between 1672 and 1675 by John Norris, 'frame-maker to the Court'. The type is known as a 'Sunderland' frame after the 2nd Earl of Sunderland (1640–1702), although it can be traced to Anglo-Dutch frames of c.1640, as for example on the Ham Staircase. There are still 22 pictures in the Gallery, and they are hung as far as possible (in the absence of any earlier evidence as to their arrangement) in the sequence described in the 1844 inventory. Hooks on the back of the frames slot into iron sockets on the walls, thus fixing the pictures at what may be their original height. With only two sources of light, at either end of the Gallery, the pictures can never have been brightly lit. To increase their visibility, copies have been made of the electric picture lights installed by the 9th Earl of Dysart before 1904.

EAST (NEAR) WALL, LEFT TO RIGHT:

After Sir ANTHONY VAN DYCK (1599–1641)
Lady Lucy Percy, Countess of Carlisle (1599–1660)
Celebrated for her beauty and political intrigues, she was one of Henrietta Maria's ladies-in-waiting, described by Charles I as 'lively and lovely, constantly entertaining'. The original is at Petworth in West Sussex.

After Sir ANTHONY VAN DYCK (1599–1641)
Queen Henrietta Maria (1609–69)*
The consort of Charles I. Dated 1637, with Queen's monogram and crown, and probably part of

The Long Gallery

21

*The Long Gallery;
watercolour by
H. W. Brewer, 1886
(private collection)*

William Murray's collection. The original is in the Royal Collection.

Attributed to JOHN WEESOP (active 1641–52)
*Elizabeth Murray, Lady Tollemache, later Countess of Dysart and Duchess of Lauderdale (1626–98)**
Painted between 1647 and 1669, when she was married to her first husband, Sir Lionel Tollemache.

Sir PETER LELY (1618–80)
*Lady Elizabeth Tollemache, Lady Lorne, later Duchess of Argyll (1659–1735)**
The eldest daughter of Elizabeth Murray and Sir Lionel Tollemache, she married Archibald, Lord Lorne, eldest son of the 9th Earl of Argyll, in 1677/8, when this picture was painted. Lord Lorne was created 1st Duke of Argyll in 1701.

After Sir ANTHONY VAN DYCK (1599–1641)
*Self-portrait**
The artist shows off a gold chain, given him by the King, and points to a sunflower, which symbolised the special relationship between art and nature, and between a faithful subject and his sovereign-cum-patron – the 'sun' which the flower always follows. The original, of 1635/6, is in the collection of the Duke of Westminster.

Sir PETER LELY (1618–80)
? Lady Katherine Murray (d.1669/70)
As this portrait bears a close resemblance to Lely's and Weesop's portraits of Elizabeth and Margaret Murray, it may represent one of the two other surviving daughters and co-heiresses of the 1st Earl of Dysart, of whom there was a portrait here in 1683.

ENGLISH, c.1630
Portrait of an Unknown Lady
This portrait is one of a group that must originally have hung at Helmingham, as it does not appear on any of the seventeenth-century Ham inventories.

After Sir ANTHONY VAN DYCK (1599–1641)
*Katherine Bruce, Mrs William Murray, later Countess of Dysart (d.1649)**
Daughter of Colonel Norman Bruce of Clackmannan, she married William Murray before 1626. After Murray, a staunch Royalist, went into exile in 1645, 'Dame Katherine' remained behind at Ham, with their four daughters.

CORNELIUS JONSON (1593–1661)
William, 2nd Duke of Hamilton (1616–51)
Signed: *Cornelius Jonson P[inxit] 1649*
He succeeded to the dukedom in March 1649, after the execution of his brother James, and was killed at

the Battle of Worcester in 1651. He wears the insignia of the Garter, awarded in 1649/50. Painted in Holland.

Sir PETER LELY (1618–80)
Elizabeth Murray, Lady Tollemache, later Countess of Dysart and Duchess of Lauderdale (1626–98) with a Blackamoor Servant
Painted c.1651, when she was married to her first husband, Sir Lionel Tollemache. The rose which the page offers her may be a symbol of fertility, since the portrait was painted about the time of the birth of her second son. Probably hung at Helmingham in the seventeenth century.

Sir PETER LELY (1618–80)
Lady Margaret Murray, Lady Maynard (c.1638–82)
The youngest daughter and co-heiress of the 1st Earl of Dysart, painted about 1670. She married the 2nd Baron Maynard of Little Easton in Essex, Comptroller of the Royal Household, in 1662. Probably hung at Helmingham in the seventeenth century.

CORNELIUS JONSON (1593–1661)
*John, Duke of Lauderdale (1616–82)**
Initialled and indistinctly dated
Painted during the Civil War years, before October 1643. The misleading inscription, as William Murray, Earl of Dysart, dates only from around 1800.

WEST WALL (SOUTH TO NORTH):

ENGLISH, 1589(?)
*Sir John Maitland, 1st Baron Maitland of Thirlestane (c.1544/5–95)**
Lord Chancellor of Scotland and grandfather of the Duke of Lauderdale. It was the model for David Paton's drawing of Maitland in the Duchess's Private Closet.

Sir ANTHONY VAN DYCK (1599–1641) and Studio
*King Charles I (1600–49)**
Almost certainly the portrait of '*Le Roi vestu de noir*' given to '*Monsr Morre*' (Murray) by the King, '*avec sa mollure*', ie in this very frame.

Sir PETER LELY (1618–80)
Portrait of an Unknown Gentleman, inscribed as Sir Henry Vane
Possibly the portrait listed in 1683 as of William, 1st Lord Alington (1610–48), first husband of Elizabeth Tollemache, eldest daughter of Sir Lionel, 2nd Bt. The sitter looks very like the regicide Sir Harry Vane the Younger (1613–62), but no portrait of

Charles I; by Anthony Van Dyck and Studio (Long Gallery). Almost certainly the portrait given to William Murray by the King and still in its original frame

him was listed in 1683, and he would be out of place at Royalist Ham.

Sir PETER LELY (1618–80)
Portrait of an Unknown Commander, inscribed as Lord Alington
A young man, painted in the 1670s, so it cannot be any Lord Alington.

Sir PETER LELY (1618–80)
? Sir Charles Compton (d.1661)
Second son of the 2nd Earl of Northampton. Like his brother, Sir William (also in the Gallery), he was a prominent Cavalier officer.

Studio of Sir PETER LELY (1618–80)
*John, Duke of Lauderdale (1616–82) in Garter Robes**
Painted after 1672, when Lauderdale was created Duke of Lauderdale and Marquess of March, and made Knight of the Garter. The original full-length is at Thirlestane Castle in Berwickshire.

After/Studio of Sir PETER LELY (1618–80)
*King Charles II (1630–85)**
The King dined at Ham in 1672.

Sir PETER LELY (1618–80) and Studio
Thomas Clifford, 1st Baron Clifford of Chudleigh (1630–73)*
Painted in 1672, when Clifford was appointed Lord Treasurer (he carries the Treasurer's wand of office). Like Lauderdale, he was a member of the Cabal, the King's inner Cabinet (1667–73).

Sir PETER LELY (1618–80)
Portrait of an Unknown Gentleman, inscribed as Tollemache, Earl of Dysart
Painted c.1660, and so cannot be the 3rd Earl of Dysart (1649–1727), as inscribed.

Sir PETER LELY (1618–80)
Sir William Compton (1625–63)*
Signed with monogram
Third son of the 2nd Marquess of Northampton, he was a distinguished Cavalier commander, and (during the Commonwealth) a leading member of the Sealed Knot. He was the second husband of Elizabeth, sister of Sir Lionel Tollemache, 3rd Bt, and thus brother-in-law to the Countess of Dysart. Painted in the 1650s.

JOHN MICHAEL WRIGHT (1617–94)
Colonel the Hon. John Russell (1620–81)*
Signed: *Io. MRitus P. 1659*
Son of 6th Earl of Bedford, he was (like Compton) a famous Royalist officer and leading member of the Sealed Knot. He was also a close friend of William Murray.

FURNITURE

In 1655 the Gallery contained 'ten long stooles' and 'Three couches' upholstered in silk. There were 'five litle tables of black Ebenie' and a billiard-table. At a time when glass was extremely expensive, the 'Three great lookinge glasses' would have been considerable status symbols. In the 1670s and subsequently, the Gallery was even more sparsely furnished. Four stools and two armchairs were the only items of seat furniture; the remainder consisted of a single cabinet, two stands, seven rose boxes, two 'Japan Screens' (in 1683 only) and four globes.

OPPOSITE DOOR FROM NORTH DRAWING ROOM:

The Japanese lacquer cabinet on a Dutch gilt stand in the form of winged putti with legs reminiscent of elephants' trunks is probably the 'Indian Cabinet wt a gilt frame carved' listed in the 1679 inventory.

(This was then the only cabinet in the gallery.) It was made in 1630–50, possibly in Kyoto.

TO LEFT AND RIGHT:

The pair of walnut and pine parcel gilt tables with legs in the form of caryatids are possibly the 'two sideboard tables' listed in 1655 in the Great Dining Room (the Hall Gallery). However, their similarity to the furniture in the Green Closet may make a date of c.1670 more likely. They have been extensively restored.

The pair of candlestands in the form of blackamoors supporting tambourines was also in the Great Dining Room, where they were described as 'Blackamore Stands' in 1683. They are Italian (probably Venetian), c.1670. On 14 December 1730 George Nix submitted a bill 'for new Gilding and Japanning 2 fine India figures'.

The pair of mahogany candlestands with tripod cabriole-legged bases are the 'Two Neat Stands made to two Stone tops The Pillars & Claws Ornamented' made by John Hele in 1744. The circular scagliola tops may have been originally part of an earlier pair of 'stands of Inlaid marble' listed here in 1679.

Six of the 'Seavon boxes carv'd and guilt for tuby roses' listed in 1679 still stand here. Their original white and gold decoration is in course of reinstatement. These small jardinières would probably have always stood in the window bays. Tuberoses are strongly scented flowers, which were popular in the seventeenth century.

The cabinets, one kingwood, the other ebony inlaid with floral marquetry, on the North Drawing Room wall are both c.1675 and either Dutch or English.

The three long stools ('Squobbs') are from a set of four (one, with its original tapestry cover, is in the Museum Room, see p.16). The bulbous legs have vestiges of chinoiserie decoration. The stools were first listed here in the Lauderdale inventories, but were probably made c.1640. The tapestry covers are extremely rare (two survive); copies have been made for the three stools on open display. In 1679 the stools were provided with case covers of 'purple and white Sarsnet', to match the curtains.

PORCELAIN

There is a massed arrangement in seventeenth-century style of Chinese blue-and-white porcelain both on the Japanese lacquer cabinet and on the two other cabinets. One vase is of late seventeenth-century Delft origin, the decoration based on a Chinese original of *c*.1640. Similar arrangements can be seen in a photograph published in 1904.

THE GREEN CLOSET

Designed to display cabinet pictures and miniatures, its scale intimate in contrast to the adjoining Long Gallery, the Green Closet is of the greatest rarity, not only as a survival from the reign of Charles I (whose own closets for the display of small works of art have long since disappeared), but also because it retains many of its seventeenth-century and later contents. In 1610 the room had a lower ceiling, which was raised when the carved woodwork and the ceiling paintings were installed by Franz Cleyn (see below) during William Murray's refurbishment of 1637–9. Architecturally, the room has remained unchanged since *c*.1672, when the door into the North Drawing Room was opened up. Previously, the only access was from the Long Gallery: it was designated the 'Closet within the gallerie' in 1655.

In 1655 the room was hung with 'greene stuffe'; the present silk damask hangings and upholstery are copies of the post-1672 'green damask', whose pattern matches the seventeenth-century damask in the Queen's Antechamber. The fringing survives from a nineteenth-century replacement of the room's textiles. The single window (a second window in the centre of the east wall was blocked either *c*.1637–9 or *c*.1672) faces north, an orientation thought desirable by contemporary theorists (with the sanction of Vitruvius) for its 'steady light'. It also has the advantage of reducing the risk of light damage. In 1679 there were 'Two window Curtaines of White damusk fring'd' and 'six green sarsnet curtaines fring'd' hanging from 'guilt Curtaine rods round the roome', which could be drawn to protect the paintings from light and dust. The table and the green upholstered seat furniture were also provided with sarsenet case-covers. Modern copies of all these decorative and practical furnishings and fittings have recently been provided.

The pictures and miniatures are hung from copies of the original gilt and lacquered pins, of which a few original examples survive. The room relied entirely upon natural light or lamps or candles brought in for occasional use. Display lighting has been enhanced by copies of the 9th Earl of Dysart's electric picture lights, installed before 1904. The 'fire pan garnished with silver' and the 'brasse fender guilt' listed in 1683 still stand in the grate.

PICTURES

The photographs of 1904 and *c*.1920 show an immensely rich hang of cabinet pictures and miniatures (since dismantled) that extended even to the sides of the chimneybreast. This was the arrangement in 1844, when 97 pictures were listed, a considerable increase since 1677, when there were 57, but the spirit of the seventeenth-century room was undoubtedly preserved. It may be that the bones of the hang (eg the upper register of ebony-framed pictures with their lower edges aligned and a concentration of miniatures below, on the long east wall) were filled out as further additions were made during the eighteenth and early nineteenth centuries. In 1677 there was a similar mix of pictures framed in gilt and ebony:

Nynteine pictures with guilt frames
Therttie eight of black Abinie frames.

The 1683 'Estimate of Pictures' reveals that 22 of the pictures then hung in the Green Closet are still at Ham and another ten, now hanging here, were also listed elsewhere in 1683. It is still possible to marshall approximately the same number of pictures as in 1677: of the 97 recorded in 1844 (of which 36 had been in the Closet in 1683), 60 are still at Ham. The 1844 arrangement has been used as a basis for the new hang, although certain fragile miniatures have had to be hung together in glazed frames.

Because the miniatures are still in course of arrangement, the following list is confined to mural and cabinet pictures.

CEILING PAINTING:

Franz Cleyn (1582–1658)
The compositions are taken, in reverse, from paintings in the Royal Collection by Polidoro da Caravaggio (*c*.1495–1543), and, as they are in tempera on paper, may initially have formed parts of tapestry cartoons for Mortlake; they recur in two panels of tapestry at Hardwick Hall, Derbyshire, woven at Hatton Garden some twenty years after Cleyn's death.

CENTRAL OVAL:

Flora with Cupids sporting among Clouds

The Green Closet; watercolour by H. W. Brewer, 1886 (private collection)

SOUTH COVE:

Putti and Cupids playing with Goats

WEST (FIREPLACE) COVE:

Satyr with a Nymph and Putto, and Cupids playing with Satyrs

NORTH COVE:

Nymphs towing a Boat with a Nymph and two Satyrs

EAST COVE:

Putti and a Cupid towing a Putto on a Cockleshell Boat

EAST WALL (OPPOSITE FIREPLACE), TOP ROW (LEFT TO RIGHT):

PIETER VERELST (1618–after 1668)
*Boors playing at Cards**
Signed: *P.Verelst 1653*

JACQUES STELLA (1596–1657)
*Salome with the head of St John the Baptist**
Signed: *Stella f. 1637*

Attributed to SIMON DE VLIEGER (c.1600–53)
*A Landscape**

JACQUES STELLA (1596–1657)
*The Virgin and Child with St John the Baptist and Child Angels**

After ADRIAEN BROUWER (1606–38)
*Boors smoking and drinking**
The original is in the Staatliche Gemäldegalerie in Kassel.

MIDDLE ROW (LEFT TO RIGHT):

NORTH ITALIAN, 1546
*Portrait of a Young Painter**
On panel; inscribed: AETATIS 18/ANNO 1546
The pose suggests this is a self-portrait.

Attributed to GERARD DOU (1613–75)
*Head of an Old Man**
On copper; bears Dou's signature: GDOU
The Dutch carved limewood frame, c.1675, is in the tradition that Grinling Gibbons grew from.

After HANS ROTTENHAMMER (1564–1625)
*Danäe and the shower of gold**
On copper
Zeus turned himself into a shower of gold to impregnate Danäe, who had been locked up in a tower by her father. The original was given to

The Green Closet in 1920

Charles I by the Earl of Ancram. William Murray gave him another Rottenhammer.

By or after FRANS POST (1612–80)
*A West Indian Plantation**
From 1637 to 1644 Post travelled to Brazil and the West Indies in the retinue of Count Johan Maurits of Nassau-Siegen, who had been sent by the Dutch West India Company to colonise north-east Brazil. Post was probably the first European to paint landscapes of the New World.

FLEMISH, mid-sixteenth-century
*Putti enacting a Bacchanalian scene**
On copper
Ascribed to an unknown 'Octava Rene' in the 1683 Estimate.

After HANS HOLBEIN the Younger (1497/8–1543)
*Head of Erasmus (c.1466–1536)**
After the head in the portrait at Longford Castle, Wiltshire. The frame is a pendant to that on the Dou.

Attributed to ADRIAEN BROUWER (1606–38)
Peasant with a Jug*
Closer to Brouwer, to whom Jan Wyck ascribed it, than to David Teniers (1610–90), to whom the Estimate gave it.

BOTTOM ROW (LEFT TO RIGHT):

After ? ANTONIUS MOR (?1519–?1575)
Purported portrait of Emperor Charles V (1500–58)

After FRANÇOIS CLOUET (c.1510–72)
Henri II of France (1519–59)

SOUTH WALL:

LEFT OF DOORWAY:

ENGLISH, second quarter of the eighteenth century
Carlo and Ubaldo removing Rinaldo from Armida
Gouache
Previously misidentified as *Agrippina landing with the Ashes of Germanicus*, it seems to have been derived from an early seventeenth-century French picture.

RIGHT OF DOORWAY:

JOSEPH GOUPY (c.1680–c.1770)
Germanicus embarking with Agrippina
Gouache
After defeating Arminius in Germany, Germanicus was sent by his uncle and adoptive father, the Emperor Tiberius, to govern Armenia and Syria. His wife Agrippina accompanied him.

JOSEPH GOUPY (c.1680–c.1770)
The Death of Germanicus
He died in Syria, probably poisoned on the orders of the Emperor Tiberius. Adapted from Poussin's celebrated painting in the Minneapolis Institute of Arts.

WEST WALL, LEFT OF CHIMNEY:

After DANIEL MYTENS (c.1590–1647/8)
James, 2nd Marquess of Hamilton, KG (1589–1625)*
Father of the 1st and 2nd Dukes of Hamilton, he was one of those behind Prince Charles's journey in Spain in 1623. The life-size original whole-length is in the Royal Collection.

AMBROSIUS BOSSCHAERT the Elder (1573–1621)
Blackbird, Butterfly and Cherries*
On panel; signed: *A. Bosschaert*
The frame is similar to those on the Great Staircase, where it originally hung.

OVER CHIMNEY:

After DANIEL MYTENS (c.1590–1647/8)
James I (1566–1625) in State Robes
The possible, life-size original of 1621 is in the National Portrait Gallery.

DUTCH, seventeenth-century (?)
Portrait of a Woman*

BARTHOLOMEUS BREENBERGH (c.1598–1657)
Landscape with Playing Satyr Children and Goats*
Formerly signed: *B. Breenbergh*

DUTCH, seventeenth-century (?)
Portrait of a Man*

RIGHT OF CHIMNEY:

After DANIEL MYTENS (c.1590–1647/8)
Ludovick Stuart, 2nd Duke of Lennox and Duke of Richmond, KG (1594–1624)*
Favourite of James I. The life-size original whole-length is at Longford Castle.

FURNITURE

The silver-mounted ebony table on caryatid supports bears in the centre of the top the monogram of

The silver-mounted ebony table, c.1670, in the Green Closet

Elizabeth Dysart, the countess's coronet dating it to 1655–72. Stylistically, the table is probably *c.*1670. Silver-mounted furniture was popular in France, and although this table was probably made in England, its design derives from engravings by Jean le Pautre (1618–82) which disseminated the Louis XIV style of Charles Le Brun. The caryatid legs are similar to the pair of stools and to the supports of the two lacquer cabinets, all of which have stood in the Green Closet since at least 1677. The stands were probably bronzed and gilded by the 6th Earl in the early nineteenth century.

The pair of Japanese lacquer cabinets c.1630 on English stands in the form of putti, c.1670, are the 'Two Japan Cabinets and Frames' listed in 1679. They were probably made in Kyoto. The bronzed and gilded decoration is probably early nineteenth-century.

THE LIBRARY CLOSET

This and the Library were part of the Duke's private suite, communicating with the Duke's Closet below by means of the stairs beyond the Library. It was described in 1674 as 'my Lords Clossett next the new Library' and was renovated in 1672–4, when double-glazing was inserted: this chilly corner room lacks a fireplace.

The Library Closet has been repainted, as originally intended, to match the seventeenth-century cedar and cedar graining used in the Library, and hung with portraits, engravings and drawings, much as it was in 1844.

PICTURES

SOUTH WALL, FLANKING WINDOWS:

D. M. MÜLLER Junior and others, purportedly after INIGO JONES (1573–1652)
Plans for a Palace of Whitehall
Tinted engravings, published in 1748 and 1749
The surviving designs for a new palace for Charles I were actually produced, and mostly after Jones's death, by his pupil John Webb (1611–72).

WEST WALL:

Design for the inscription on the coffin-plate of Anna Maria, wife of the 6th Earl of Dysart, d.14 September, 1804, aged 59
Black ink

LUKE SULLIVAN after WILLIAM HOGARTH (1697–1762)
The March of the Guards towards Scotland in 1745
Hand-coloured engraving, published in 1750

NORTH WALL:

Ascribed to THOMAS HUDSON (1701–79)
? *John Carteret, 2nd Lord Carteret and 2nd Earl Granville (1690–1763)*
Inscribed and dated 1739
Walpole's leading opponent in the House of Lords between 1730 and 1742, and father of Grace Carteret, wife of the 4th Earl of Dysart.

THOMAS BADESLADE (*c.*1715–50) and JOHN ROCQUE (*c.*1704–62)
Ham House and grounds
Engraving
Published in *Vitruvius Britannicus* (1739).

JAMES BASIRE (1730–1802) after EDWARD EDWARDS (1738–1806)
The Field of Cloth of Gold
Hand-coloured engraving, 1774
After a watercolour made in 1771 from the oil painting in the Royal Collection.

ENGLISH, *c.*1671/2
The South Front of Ham House
Possibly an architect's design for Ham's new south front, erected in 1672–4, under the supervision of William Samwell.

Attributed to JOHN SLEZER (d.1714) and JAN WYCK (*c.*1640–1702)
Perspective view of Ham House from the South, c.1671–2
Pen, ink and watercolour with graphite
Slezer was a German engineer and surveyor employed by Lauderdale at Thirlestane Castle, and Wyck was a Dutch artist who did several inset paintings at Ham. This drawing may represent a design proposal for the new south front and formal garden, built in 1672–4.

EAST WALL:

LEFT OF DOOR:

JACOB HOUBRAKEN (1698–1780) after Sir GODFREY KNELLER, Bt (1646/9–1723)
Lt. Gen. Thomas Tollemache in armour (c.1651–94)
Engraving
The Duchess's younger son. After the painting now in the Hall Gallery.

Attributed to JOHN SLEZER (d.1714) and JAN
WYCK (c.1640–1702)
Plan of Ham House and gardens c.1671–2
Pen, ink and wash with graphite
Slezer produced several similar plans of proposed
alterations for the Duke of Lauderdale's Scottish
castles, usually under the direction of the Scottish
architect Sir William Bruce. The Ham plan shows
the new south wing (built as drawn) and an
elaborate formal garden (which may not have been
completed exactly to this design).

ABOVE DOOR:

ENGLISH, late seventeenth-century
Two Children and a Dog

RIGHT OF DOOR:

JACOB HOUBRAKEN (1698–1780) after Sir PETER
LELY (1618–80)
John, Duke of Lauderdale (1616–82)
Engraving; dated 1740
Done, in reverse, from the image in the double
portrait in the Hall Gallery. Given by Mr H. Ball-
Wilson (former owner of Ham House stable block)
in 1978, in memory of his wife.

ENGLISH, c.1830
Ham House from the North
Watercolour
The north elevation of the house in about 1825.
It may have been painted for Barbara Holland's
Richmond and its surrounding scenery (1832), illus-
trated by J.D.Harding, G.Barnard and other
artists.

After THOMAS ROWLANDSON (1756–1827)
Miss Worthy's marriage, Dr Syntax in the chair
Coloured aquatint
Ham House is seen in the background.

FURNITURE

The cabinet (in the form of a chest on chest) veneered
with walnut and kingwood is c.1675.

THE LIBRARY

The Library was constructed in 1672–4, when the
shelves from the 'old Library' (the Queen's Antechamber) were moved here and an additional 572
feet of shelving 'wth Cedar mouldings about them'
was fitted before March 1673. Henry Harlow, the

joiner, also supplied 'the seder table and drawers In
My Lords Librarie' at a cost of £12 (this is the
writing-desk still *in situ*). The plasterer Henry Wells
in 1674 charged for '25 yards of frettwork in ye
library at six shill. six pence ye yard'. His elaborate
plaster ceiling has been recently repainted in a deep
warm tone compatible with the cedar graining of
the bookshelves.

The Duke of Lauderdale was erudite. The sale
catalogues of his library (sold between 1688 and
1692) reveal that it was rich in Italian, French and
Spanish works, including books on architecture, the
arts, gardening and medicine. The 3rd and 4th Earls
of Dysart were also bibliophiles, but their collections were sold in 1938. The Library has been newly
furnished with books bequeathed to the Trust by
the late Norman Norris of Brighton. In 1844 there
were 'scarlet ground festoon curtins', which were
probably put up in the mid-eighteenth century by
the 4th Earl of Dysart.

FURNITURE

The terrestrial and celestial globes, c.1746, are signed by
Johan Senex, and are still covered with the gilt-
tooled leather case-covers supplied by him in 1746.
Similar leather case-covers may be seen in the
Museum Room (see p.16) and were standard issue
for fine furniture, though it is extremely unusual for
them to have survived. In 1679 there were 'Two
great and two Small Globes' in the Long Gallery;
these must be replacements.

The mahogany pole-screens on tripod stands, have as
their banners circular glazed maps. One is probably
the 'round map screen' supplied by Samuel Wil-
liams 'At the Golden Lyon & Ball in St Paul's
Church Yard' in 1743. They were bought back for
Ham in 1991 with a grant from the Monument
Trust.

*The pair of cedarwood armchairs with claw feet and
carved finials on the splat and arms,* c.1675, is part of the
original furniture of the Library, being the 'Two
Arme Chaires of Cedar' listed in 1677.

The library steps, of oak with brass handles, were
presumably installed by the 4th Earl of Dysart
c.1740.

SCULPTURE

*The 'Three Plaister figures of Milton, Dryden and
Shakespeare'* listed in 1844, of plaster painted to look
like bronze, are after models by John Cheere (1709–

The Library

87). Another version of the Milton is dated 1749; the 'Dryden' is in fact a depiction of the poet Spenser, *c*.1750; the Shakespeare, *c*.1750, is copied from the monument in Westminster Abbey by Scheemakers (1740). All three were acquired by the 4th Earl of Dysart in 1756.

THE QUEEN'S ANTECHAMBER

Previously 'the ould Library', and converted into an antechamber to the adjacent Queen's Bedchamber in 1673–4. At first, it was called the 'Green Drawing Roome' after its green velvet hangings, but between 1679 and 1683 it assumed its present name and acquired the present set of wall-coverings. It is remarkable for the fact that it is still 'Hunge with foure peices of blewe Damusk [now faded to brown], impaned and bordered wth. blew velvet embroidered wth. gould and fringed' and for what is probably the original olivewood graining on a gilt ground. The walls were originally protected by case curtains of 'yealow stript Indian Sarsnet'. The two window curtains, of 'white Indian Damusk fringed wth. silke', hung from gilt curtain rods; both have recently been replaced by modern copies. The fire-irons (and even the rod half sunk into the hearth) were all 'garnished with Silver', an indication of the importance of the room as a prelude to the richness of the Queen's Bedchamber.

PICTURES

WEST WALL (INSET OVER DOOR):

DIRCK VAN DEN BERGEN (1640–95)
A Landscape with Herdsfolk and Ruins
These three pictures were painted for this room between 1677 and 1679.

EAST WALL (INSET OVER FIREPLACE):

DIRCK VAN DEN BERGEN (1640–95)
Landscape with a Herdsman leading an Ass

31

The Queen's Antechamber

EAST WALL (INSET OVER DOOR):

DIRCK VAN DEN BERGEN (1640–95)
A Lion Hunt

FURNITURE

The lacquer cabinet on a giltwood stand is probably the 'Japan cabinet wth. a carved guilt frame' which was in the bedroom above the Chapel (the Museum Room) in 1683. The base is English or Dutch (probably the latter), *c.*1675; the cabinet is of incised seventeenth-century Japanese lacquer (taken from a screen) probably made up in Europe.

The lacquer chairs survive from 1679 and once formed part of a larger set: 'Twelve back stooles (wth. Cane bottomes) Japaned' were listed here in 1683; they were originally provided with cushions matching the wall-hangings. There are three similar designs of this type of furniture still at Ham. They are probably English, of beechwood japanned in imitation of Japanese lacquer; the initials ED (for Elizabeth Dysart) beneath a Duchess's coronet on the splat, indicate that she sometimes chose to retain her own title as a countess in her own right, even after her marriage to the Duke of Lauderdale in 1672. These chairs may have been among the 24 'Cane bottome backe stooles' purchased from John Dutton in 1673.

The lacquer side-table, *c.*1675, is probably Dutch. It is highly unusual because the incised lacquer, which looks convincingly Chinese, was in fact made in Europe.

The lacquer close-stool, *c.*1675, has stood here since 1679. Of oak, japanned in imitation of oriental lacquer and inlaid with mother-of-pearl, its hinges are original, terminating (like the keyhole escutcheons) with ducal coronets.

PORCELAIN

In the seventeenth century, coloured Chinese porcelain was rarer and more expensive than blue-and-white. The three pieces on the chimneypiece are very early Qing dynasty, c.1660. This decoration is known as *Wucai* (five colour). The other china, particularly that on the cabinet, is of a slightly later version of this colouring known in Europe as *famille verte* and is c.1700. The single baluster vase with trumpet neck, c.1730, has an early example of the *famille rose* glaze.

THE QUEEN'S BEDCHAMBER

In the Lauderdales' time, this was the most magnificent room in the house and the climax of the series of rooms forming the State Apartment. Already known by this name in 1673, it must have been prepared in that year for a visit by Queen Catherine of Braganza. Presumably, in her honour, it was provided with a bed 'made in Portugall' for use in summer: the furniture and hangings were changed according to the season, the 'Winter furniture'

being designed, not surprisingly, for warmth. The decoration of the room, with its gilded crowns over the chimneypiece and on the piers, emphasised its regal status, as did its position at the centre of the south front. Outside, as in a royal palace, the axis of the garden and of the avenues beyond emphasised the pivotal position of the State Bedchamber.

Entering from the Antechamber, the visitor would have faced a State Bed richly hung with silk (cloth of gold and velvet in the winter), placed in the centre of the opposite wall, upon the parquet of a dais set in French style behind a balustrade. The elaborate parquetry at that end of the room survives (though now on a level with the rest of the floor), as do the woodwork (carved in 1673 by John Bullimore and gilded by Nicholas Moore), the plasterwork ceiling (probably by Henry Wells) and the marble fireplace with its overmantel after Andrea del Sarto. Originally, the walls were hung with 'Rich Tapestry wth gold in them of the seasons of ye yeare'. The silver-mounted chimney furniture survives; the mounts of the fire-pan incorporate the Lauderdales' ducal cipher.

In the parquetry, on either side of where the bed stood, are the monograms of the Lauderdales in 'Cedar inlaid with wallnutt tree', which were made by Henry Harlow at a cost of 35s a square yard. This was preserved by the 4th Earl, who converted the

The Queen's Bedchamber; watercolour by H. W. Brewer, 1886 (private collection)

The Queen's Bedchamber

room into a drawing-room in *c.*1744 and who commissioned much of the present furniture and the tapestries from William Bradshaw (d.1775), a London weaver, cabinetmaker and upholsterer.

PICTURES

WEST WALL (INSET OVER DOOR):

DIRCK VAN DEN BERGEN (1640–95)
A Pair of Lions with a Leopard in a Cave
Painted, with the two other overdoors, for this room by 1677.

NORTH WALL (INSET OVER FIREPLACE):

After ANDREA DEL SARTO (1486–1530)
The Virgin and Child with St John
After the lost fresco of the Porta Pinti in Florence. Here by 1677.

EAST WALL (INSET OVER DOOR):

DIRCK VAN DEN BERGEN (1640–95)
A Landscape with a Shepherdess under an awning

FURNITURE

The giltwood pier-glasses and tables were supplied by William Bradshaw, whose bill was paid on 5 May 1743. They are described as 'a pair of fine gilt carved marble tables with a pair of oval glasses with carved frames richly gilt'.

The fruitwood chairs and sofa upholstered in red, green and cream silk velvet, *c.*1730, are part of a larger set which was split between this room and the North Drawing Room. The velvet upholstery, in remarkably good condition, was woven in Genoa, Lyons or Spitalfields. Bradshaw supplied case-covers in 'crimson lutestring [a glossy silk]' in 1744.

The commode, elaborately inlaid with rosewood, satinwood and other woods and with ormolu mounts, is attributed to Georg Haupt (1741–84) and Christopher Fuhrlohg (*c.*1740–*c.*1787), Swedish cabinetmakers, both resident in London by 1768. They spent the previous four years in Paris, and this virtuoso piece of *c.*1770 is most closely comparable to a commode signed by P. A. Foullet. It is probably identifiable with the 'very curious inlaid and gilt pier commode' listed in 1844; its original leather case-cover is still at Ham.

The harpsichord is dated 1634 and although it bears the name of the famous maker Johannes (Jan) Ruckers of Antwerp, it was probably made in London *c.*1730. Flemish harpsichords, especially those by the Ruckers family, were highly prized in the eighteenth century and were often extended to provide a greater musical range. This instrument is masquerading as a stretched harpsichord of this kind and was clearly built as a deliberate forgery. Handel's favourite harpsichord was by Ruckers.

The silk and wool tapestries, *c.*1735, are composed of figures and motifs from paintings by Watteau and Pater. They were woven by Bradshaw, 'tapestry weaver in Soho Square', whose signature, in prominent capitals, can be seen in the lower right-hand corner of the tapestry on the left wall. The subjects (from left to right) are *The Dance*, *The Fountain*, *The Swing* and *The Fruit-gatherer*.

THE QUEEN'S CLOSET

As its name implies, this was a private room for the use of the Queen or other occupant of the adjoining bedchamber, and only the most high-ranking guests would have been admitted.

Completed in 1673, the elaborate carving is by John Bullimore and the parquet floor is by Henry Harlow, who again decorated it with the ducal Lauderdale cipher and coronet, a motif repeated also on the scagliola chimneypiece and window-sill, both by a Roman craftsman, Baldassare Artima. This richly decorated room is exceptional for the survival of almost all of its original décor, although the marbling, originally 'white and vaind', has been repainted and the window curtain of 'white Indian Damusk' has been copied. Otherwise all is intact, including the winter hangings of 'Crimson and gould stuff bordered wth. green and gould and silver stuff', which were originally protected by case-curtains of 'Crimson Sarsenet' hung from gilt rods matching the rod at the window.

PICTURES

INSET OVER DOOR AND FIREPLACE:

THOMAS WYCK (*c.*1616–77)
Two Capriccios of Seaports and a View of the Bay of Naples, all with Orientals and an Antique Statue
All three signed: *T. Wijk*
Here by 1677.

CEILING PAINTING:

ANTONIO VERRIO (*c.*1639–1707)
Ganymede and the Eagle
Zeus transformed himself into an eagle to carry off Ganymede, a beautiful young shepherd who became his cupbearer on Mount Olympus.

FURNITURE

The gilt armchair upholstered en suite with the wall-hangings is one of two (the other is in the Museum Room, see p.16) described in 1679 as 'Two sleeping chayres carv'd and guilt frames covered wth. Crimson and gould stuff wth. gould fringe'. Placed on the dais, these would have fulfilled the role of thronelike 'chairs of estate', but with their adjustable backs were also designed for 'reposeing' in comfort and privacy.

The two gilt stools, *c.*1675, are more properly termed *carreaux*, the humblest pieces of furniture in a grand setting. They are probably the 'Two small squob frames carv'd and guilt' listed in the Queen's Bedchamber in 1683, which would have been placed at the foot of the State Bed. They may have been made by Jean Poitevin, who supplied a State Bed with two *carreaux en suite* in 1673. The cushions are modern copies.

The visitor now returns downstairs to the Great Hall and enters the Marble Dining Room.

THE MARBLE DINING ROOM

Like the early seventeenth-century Great Dining Room (the Hall Gallery) upstairs, this room was also a salon for receptions, placed centrally with the Duke and Duchess's apartments leading off to either side. Its principal role was for dining on a more intimate scale than in the upstairs banqueting room. The name, dating from at least 1677, recalls the black and white marble floor laid in 1673,

*The Marble
Dining Room*

of which the step into the Great Hall is all that survives.

The floor was laid with parquet probably at the same time that the original polychrome leather hangings (a section is in the Museum Room) were replaced by the present stamped and gilded leather, supplied by John Sutton, 'Leather Gilder', in 1756. This was due to the 4th Earl, who preserved the sideboard alcoves, the overdoors and the rest of the décor, revealing an antiquarian side to his more usual alterations in contemporary style. It is intended to hang copies of the crimson worsted damask festoon curtains recorded in 1844, and which probably formed part of the 4th Earl's decorative scheme.

Oval arrangements of food are shown in engravings of early table layouts. The dishes would be grouped close together in concentric ovals with a tiered circular centrepiece as in *A dinner for the King* (several of which were given at Ham) published in 1730. Guests would be helped by servants who would also replenish the glasses from stocks of wine on the sideboard or cooling in the marble cistern beneath. Dinner, the main meal of the day, was served in the Lauderdales' time at about 2 o'clock.

Depending on the importance of the occasion, the number of courses would have varied (usually two to three), as would the number of dishes per course (between five and 30). Fish, game, meat and poultry were served together, sometimes with sweet puddings, but usually these were kept for the final course, which would have included fresh fruit in season.

PICTURES

EAST WALL (INSET OVER FIREPLACE):

THOMAS HEWART after an unknown Dutch artist
Rose, the Royal Gardener, presenting a Pineapple to Charles II
The pineapple was not grown in England until the eighteenth century. The scene must be symbolic, since the setting is in Holland and Charles II never returned there after the Restoration. An inscription on the reverse states that this copy was executed by Thomas Hewart, aged twenty, in 1787. Probably copied from the prime version of this composition, which was owned by Horace Walpole, whose niece married the 5th Earl of Dysart.

EAST WALL (INSET OVER DOOR):

After POLIDORO DA CARAVAGGIO (c.1495–1543)
Putti and Cupids playing with Swans
One of four in this room of a set of six copies after paintings bought by Charles I in 1637, and now at Hampton Court. Installed here between 1677 and 1679.

WEST WALL (INSET OVER DOOR):

After POLIDORO DA CARAVAGGIO (c.1495–1543)
Putti and Cupids playing with Goats

WEST WALL:

Attributed to FRANS SNYDERS (1579–1657)
Fighting Cocks and Hens
Probably bought by the 4th Earl of Dysart when the room was redecorated in the 1750s.

SOUTH WALL (INSET OVER ALCOVE):

After POLIDORO DA CARAVAGGIO (c.1495–1543)
Nymphs towing a Boat with a Nymph and two Satyrs

SOUTH WALL (INSET OVER DOOR):

Manner of HIERONYMUS BOSCH (1460–1518)
The Harrowing of Hell
A later imitation of Bosch. Various versions of the subject exist.

SOUTH WALL (INSET OVER ALCOVE):

After POLIDORO DA CARAVAGGIO (c.1495–1543)
Putti and a Cupid pulling in a Net with a Putto on a Cockleshell Boat

FURNITURE

The caned chairs are English, c.1675, and, apart from one, are not Ham pieces but on loan from the V & A. In 1679 there were 'Eighteen carv'd Chayres of walnuttre wth Cane bottomes', and in 1683 'Two Chayres for Children'. These would have stood against the walls when not in use.

The oval gate-leg table of cedarwood, c.1675, was one of three such tables in 1679, all provided 'with leather covers'. The gate-leg form made it easy to set the tables against the wall when not in use, and their oval shape was convenient for servants as well as intimate for the diners.

IN ALCOVES:

The pair of sideboard tables, c.1675, are the 'two sideboards of Cedar wt. leather covers' listed in 1679.

BELOW:

The white marble wine-cooler is probably Dutch, c.1670, and is the 'marble sisterne' listed in 1677. It would have been filled with ice to chill white wine and other liquids. The black marble wine-cooler was originally in the Back Parlour.

The pair of giltwood pier-glasses, c.1730, were additions of the 4th Earl. The matching pier-tables, of gilt gesso with lacquer tops, are no longer at Ham.

PORCELAIN

The blue-and-white porcelain is Kangxi, c.1700.

ON SIDEBOARD TABLES:

The glass coolers are modelled after European late seventeenth-century silver Monteiths.

THE DUKE AND DUCHESS'S APARTMENTS

Disposed symmetrically as *enfilades* on either side of the Marble Dining Room between 1672 and 1674, each comprises an antechamber, bedchamber and closet. The arrangement survives remarkably intact, apart from the 4th Earl's mid-eighteenth-century conversion of the Duke's bedroom into a drawing-room (the Volury Room).

THE WITHDRAWING ROOM

After eating in the Marble Dining Room, the company would have 'withdrawn' to this room, which also served as an ante-room to the Duke's bedchamber beyond. Hung with damask, described as 'red' or 'Crimson' with a 'gold colour and Crimson fringe' (the present hangings are modern with an over-large pattern), the 'Eight arme chayres wth guilt and painted frames' (1679) were upholstered to match. The large number of chairs (eleven in 1677) reflects the use of the room for post-prandial relaxation. There was also a 'Cedar tea table'.

PICTURES

In 1679, as well as the inset pictures, there were 'Foure pictures wth. gilt Carv'd frames' and 'Eight Pictures with ebony frames' which were hung decoratively 'wth. Silk strings'. These would have had decorative bows and tassels, just as the 'great looking glasse' was adorned with 'strings & tassells'. The furnishing accounts reveal the great cost of the numerous tassels made for pictures, mirrors, curtains and upholstery, many of which were woven in gold and silver.

WEST WALL (INSET OVER DOOR):

After POLIDORO DA CARAVAGGIO (c.1495–1543)
Cupids and Putti playing Croquet and other games
This and the other overdoor were here by 1677, and are the other two copies of pictures in the Royal Collection.

WEST WALL:

Attributed to CORNELIUS JONSON (1593–1661)
Portrait of an Unknown Young Man
Apparently painted in Holland, to which Jonson retired from England in October 1643; so perhaps a friend of Lauderdale's there, though not recorded here in the eighteenth century. It has been given an elaborate mid-eighteenth-century frame in keeping with others in the house.

NORTH WALL (LEFT OF FIREPLACE):

After Sir PETER PAUL RUBENS (1577–1640)
*Faun and Bacchante**
One of a number of copies of this composition.

THOMAS WYCK (1616–77)
*An Alchemist**
Signed: *T.Wijk*
Thomas and his son Jan supplied pictures for Ham in the 1670s, both fixed and hanging. Thomas specialised in painting alchemists' laboratories, and Italianate street and harbour scenes, while Jan concentrated on battle scenes and decorative landscapes.

NORTH WALL (INSET OVER FIREPLACE):

ABRAHAM CORNELIS BEGEYN, known as BEGA (1637–97)
Landscape with Plants, Insects and a Squirrel
Signed: *A Bega fec[it]*
Formerly over the chimney in the 'Gentlewoman's Chamber' (now an office), and moved to this position in 1948.

NORTH WALL (RIGHT OF FIREPLACE):

ABRAHAM BLOEMAERT (1564–c.1651)
*The Baptism of Christ**
An early, Mannerist picture by this influential artist, reframed for the 4th Earl.

EAST WALL:

? After THOMAS WYCK (1616–77)
Capriccio of a Mediterranean Seaport with Orientals and an Antique Statue
Either a pastiche of the pictures in the Queen's Closet, or very heavily restored.

After PIER FRANCESCO MOLA (1612–66)
Hagar and Ishmael
Bought by the 4th Earl of Dysart at Lord Cholmondeley's sale, 1748. The figures are taken from a reversed engraving of one of many versions of this subject ascribed to Mola, now in the Louvre.

EAST WALL (OVER DOOR):

After POLIDORO DA CARAVAGGIO (c.1495–1543)
A Nymph, Cupids and Satyrs

FURNITURE

The cabinet on stand inlaid with ebony, tortoiseshell and marble, the interior mounted with gilt-bronze figures was probably made in Antwerp in the 1630s. It was listed in the Volury Room (the Duke's bedroom) in the Lauderdale inventories.

The upholstered armchairs with lacquered and gilt carved frames are part of a set of ten, now with various kinds of 1970s upholstery. They were originally next door in the Volury Room, where they were described in 1679 as 'Tenn arme Chayres black and guilded'.

The looking glass and pier-table flanked by candlesticks may be the 'glasse table and stands of Japan' listed in 1683. The incised lacquer is seventeenth-century Chinese. The bases of the table and candlesticks were probably replaced by John Hele in 1741.

PORCELAIN

There are massed arrangements of blue-and-white Kangxi porcelain on the ebony and tortoiseshell cabinet and on the chimneypiece.

IN FRONT OF FIREPLACE ON FLOOR:

The large vase is late sixteenth- or early seventeenth-century Ming.

UNDER TABLE OPPOSITE:

The large bottle-shaped vase is late eighteenth-century in the Ming style.

THE VOLURY ROOM

Previously called the Yellow Bedchamber, the Volury Room had acquired its name by at least 1683 from its birdcages, which were constructed in 1672–4 flanking the bay window; they were fitted with lead 'sisternes' for drinking water. Henry Harlow, the joiner, was paid the huge sum of £56 'for 4 birdcages on ye garden side' in 1673. One of Barlow's avian overdoors is dated 1673, so birds were already a theme when the bedchamber was constructed in 1672–4, first for the Duchess's use, then (after 1677) for the Duke's. The panelling was painted 'white and veined 4 times' in 1673–4, and the walls were hung with yellow (1677), and yellow and blue (1679) fringed silk, complementary to the yellow hangings of the bed. The black and gold chairs (still *in situ*) were upholstered to match.

This decoration was removed by the 4th Earl, who created a drawing-room in the 1740s. His pier-glasses and tables are still in place. His other furnishings – a set of Flemish late seventeenth-century tapestries after Poussin, and a suite of X-frame velvet-upholstered gilt sofas and chairs in the style of William Kent of *c.*1730 – will be reinstated here after conservation. The reupholstered bed placed here *c.*1970 was probably made in the 1730s to stand in the alcove of the Duchess's Bedchamber and will be returned there (see p.45). The bed-hangings, wall-hangings and the upholstery were renewed *c.*1970.

PICTURES

WEST WALL (INSET OVER DOOR):

FRANCIS BARLOW (1626–1702)
Goose with its Young, and other Birds
Signed: *F. Barlow 1673*
This and the other overdoor were probably installed in 1673 as appropriate decoration for a bird room.

EAST WALL (OVER CHIMNEY):

ENGLISH, *c.*1640
John Maitland, 1st Earl of Lauderdale (d.1645)*
A prominent Scottish peer, Lauderdale was successively a Lord of Session, Commissioner of Taxes and President of Parliament. Only son and heir of John, 1st Baron Maitland of Thirlestane, he inherited the ancient Maitland estates of Thirlestane, Lethington, Haddington and Lauder. He was succeeded by his eldest son, the future Duke of Lauderdale.

*The Volury Room
in 1920*

EAST WALL (INSET OVER DOOR):

FRANCIS BARLOW (1626 1702)
An Owl being mobbed by other Birds

FURNITURE

*The bed, c.*1730, of pine and oak partly upholstered in 1730s crimson velvet, stands on gilded feet of *c.*1670 which could have been taken from one of the important Ham beds described in the Lauderdale inventories.

*The ebonised and gilded armchairs, c.*1675, are from a set of ten described here in 1679 as 'Tenn arme Chayes black and guilded'.

The parcel-gilt pier-glasses and tables are *c.*1740.

PORCELAIN

ON CHIMNEYPIECE:

The three bowls are Kangxi; the pair with formal lotus decoration also bear the mark of the Kangxi Emperor (reigned 1662–1722), which is comparatively uncommon in pieces made for export. They are of sufficiently high quality to have been made for the Court.

THE WHITE CLOSET

This room and the adjoining private closet was the Duchess's inner sanctum where she could entertain her friends, write, read and surround herself with small works of art. This first room was called the 'White Closet' in 1677 after its painted marbling and its hangings of 'white tabby [silk] with silver fring'. In 1679 'sad' (ie grey) damask was put up, which was copied in 1980–1. The 1679 furniture included 'One Indian furnace for tee garnish'd with silver', which stood on a 'Cedar table', and in 1683 there was 'One Childs Chayre guilt'.

PICTURES

WEST WALL (INSET OVER DOOR):

DIRCK VAN DEN BERGEN (1640–90)
Landscape with Mercury and Battus
This and the other overdoor were in place by 1677.

(Right) Katherine Bruce, Countess of Dysart; attributed to Hubert Le Sueur, c.1635 (White Closet)

INSET OVER FIREPLACE:

? HENRY DANCKERTS (*c.*1625–*c.*1679)
*Ham House from the South, c.*1675–9

NORTH WALL (OVER DOOR):

BENEDETTO GENNARI (1633–1715)
Head of St Paul*
A Bolognese artist who had worked for the French court, Gennari was in England from 1674 to 1688. The majority of his English commissions were portraits and religious works for a predominantly Catholic clientele. The Duke of Lauderdale sat for a three-quarter-length portrait (now at Helmingham). This small picture was displayed with a group of four other 'heads' in the White Closet.

EAST WALL (INSET OVER WINDOW):

DIRCK VAN DEN BERGEN (1640–90)
Landscape with Nursing Herdswoman, Sleeping Herdsman, and Animals

CEILING PAINTING:

ANTONIO VERRIO (c.1639–1707)

CENTRAL OVAL: *Divine Wisdom presiding over the Liberal Arts*

COVE: *Cupids with medallions of the four Cardinal Virtues, and Sphinxes*

FURNITURE

In 1683 there were 'Six arme Cane Chayres Japanned'; these do not survive at Ham, but were complementary to the japanned furniture of the Duchess's Private Closet.

The writing-cabinet veneered with kingwood and mounted in silver, c.1675, is English, probably by a royal cabinetmaker. It was described here in 1683: 'One Scriptore of Prince wood garnished with silver'.

SCULPTURE

OVERMANTEL:

Attributed to HUBERT LE SUEUR (c.1585–1658)
Katherine Bruce, Countess of Dysart (d.1649)
Gilt bronze
The wife of William Murray, she remained throughout the Civil War at Ham, where she brought up their four daughters. Le Sueur, initially employed by the French Crown, probably came to England c.1625 in the train of Queen Henrietta Maria. This bust is contemporary with his gilt bronze head of Charles I, c.1635 (Stourhead, Wiltshire). Listed here in 1677 and described in 1683 as 'One brasse head of her Graces mother', it has always stood 'over the Chimney'. The socle is cast with the crest of the Bruce family: a tree issuing from an earl's coronet.

THE DUCHESS'S PRIVATE CLOSET

The second of the Duchess's private rooms, and called 'her Grace's Private Closet' in the various Lauderdale inventories, this was where she kept her books, her tea and some of her valuables: 'Two cases of shelves for bookes, Japanned', 'One bible with ye book of Common prayer', 'One Japan box for sweetmeats and tea' and one 'little strong box with guilt hinges' were listed at various times. Much of

The Duchess's Private Closet in 1920

the furniture was lacquered in eastern style: the Orient being the source of tea, it must have seemed appropriate to provide an exotic setting for imbibing it.

The furniture is original to the room, and the walls are hung with a modern interpretation (c.1985) of the 1683 hangings, 'Dark Mohayre bordered with flowered Silke with purple & gold fringe'. The walls were thickly hung with pictures: seventeen in ebony and four in gilt frames. The jib door communicates with a servants' staircase, and provides a short cut to the Great Hall.

PICTURES

INSET OVER FIREPLACE:

WILLIAM GOUW FERGUSON (1632/3–after 1695)
Medea casting spells among Ruined Sculpture
Installed by 1677.

INSET OVER DOOR:

WILLIAM GOUW FERGUSON (1632/3–after 1695)
Capriccio of Classical Ruins
Also in place by 1677.

41

CEILING PAINTING:

ANTONIO VERRIO (c.1639–1707)
The Penitent Magdalen, surrounded by Putti holding emblems of Time, Death and Eternity
The imagery is exceptional in England at this period, and its use in the Duchess's inner sanctum strongly suggests that she had Catholic leanings.

NORTH WALL AT TOP:

EDMUND ASHFIELD (active 1669–76)
John, Duke of Lauderdale (1616–82)*
Initialled: *E A F 1674/5*
Probably a pupil of Michael Wright, Ashfield was the first English artist to specialise in pastel portraiture.

MIDDLE REGISTER:

VENETIAN, sixteenth-century
St Sebastian*
Valued at £25 in 1683. The high price reflects the optimistic attribution (recorded on the frame) to 'Leonard Davinshaw' – Leonardo da Vinci.

DAVID PATON (active c.1668–1708) after ANDREA DEL SARTO (1486–1530)
The Holy Family (?Rest on the Flight into Egypt)*
After Sarto's fresco in the cloister of SS Annunziata in Florence. Paton was the leading draughtsman in Scotland in the seventeenth century. He produced over twenty ink on vellum drawings for the Duke and Duchess of Lauderdale, thirteen of which survive at Ham. In the 1670s he accompanied William Tollemache, the Duchess's youngest son, on his Grand Tour.

VENETIAN, sixteenth-century
St Anthony Abbot*
Pendant to the *St Sebastian*.

BOTTOM REGISTER:

DAVID PATON (active c.1668–1708)
Sir John Maitland, 1st Baron Maitland of Thirlestane (c.1544/5–95)*
After the painting of the Duke's grandfather in the Long Gallery.

DAVID PATON (active c.1668–1708) after a follower of RAPHAEL (1483–1520)
Virgin and Child with St John the Baptist*
Signed: *D. Paton fecit 1668*
After a miniature after the Bankes Madonna at Kingston Lacy, Dorset.

St Sebastian; by an unknown sixteenth-century Venetian artist (Duchess's Private Closet)

DAVID PATON (active c.1668–1708)
John Maitland, 1st Earl of Lauderdale (d.1645)*
After the painting of the Duke's father in the Volury Room.

FURNITURE

The japanned chairs, the splats decorated with a countess's coronet, c.1675, are probably the same as the 'Six Japan'd backstooles with Cane bottomes' listed in 1683, when they had cushions matching the wall-hangings.

The tea-table is a composite piece of c.1675. The upper section is Javanese, made to take tea sitting cross-legged in the customary manner; it is supported on an Anglo-Dutch base which was made to bring it up to a convenient height. This is the table described as 'Japanned' in the 1683 inventory.

The writing-cabinet with oysterwork veneer in king-wood, *c*.1675, is similar (apart from the wood) to the 'Scriptore of walnut tree' listed here in 1683.

PORCELAIN

In 1844 this room was described as the 'China Closet' and, judging by early photographs, it had become a storeroom for the Duchess of Lauderdale's extensive collection of blue-and-white porcelain, now sadly dispersed.

UNDER WRITING CABINET:

The tall bottle is Kangxi, *c*.1700.

ON TEA-TABLE:

The two cups and saucers are early eighteenth-century.

The white crackled teapot is seventeenth-century, with late seventeenth-century silver-gilt mounts (probably English). The slightly pink tinge spreading through the crackle was probably caused by many years of hot tea seeping through the glaze. By tradition, this was the Duchess of Lauderdale's personal teapot. It was presented to the National Trust through the National Art Collections Fund in 1994, by Ronald Lee, in memory of his wife.

Having returned along the enfilade and back through the Marble Dining Room, the visitor reaches the Duke's Dressing Room.

THE DUKE'S DRESSING ROOM

Completed in 1674, this served as an ante-room to the adjoining bedchamber which was originally the Duke's, but after 1677, was used by the Duchess. Both, however, retained their ancilliary rooms at opposite ends of the *enfilade* – a rather curious arrangement. Here, the Duke would have dressed and afterwards would have turned to business or relaxation. The useful furniture included in 1679 two 'Scriptores [writing-cabinets] of walnut tree' and a walnut 'writing box'. There was also a 'Cedar Close stoole box' which would probably have stood in the recess, masked by a jib door, to the left of the fireplace. Most of the furniture was

The Duke's Dressing Room

ebony, matching the black marble fireplace, and the room was hung first with 'hair Colloured Damask' [ie light brown], but by 1679 this was replaced by 'Crimson & gould colour Damask Hangings' with 'black & gould fringe'. The present modern hangings are in a single colour; the intention is to replace them with a two-colour damask as originally.

PICTURES

WEST WALL (INSET OVER DOOR):

HENRY DANCKERTS (c.1625–c.1679)
River Landscape with Classical Ruins and a Castle
Already in place by 1677, with the other overdoor.

WEST WALL:

JAKOB DE WET (1610–after 1675)
*The Hosts of Pharaoh engulfed by the Red Sea**
Signed: *J. d. Wet*
By a pupil, or close follower, of Rembrandt.

FRANCESCO BASSANO (1549–92)
*The Israelites gathering manna**
A related picture, from the circle of Francesco's father, Jacopo, is at the Schloss Ambras in the Tyrol.

NORTH WALL:

FRANCESCO BASSANO (1549–92)
*Orpheus charming the Animals**
The rare surviving early seventeenth-century frame suggests it may have been part of William Murray's collection.

Attributed to JACOPO (1510–92) and FRANCESCO (1549–92) BASSANO
*Daniel in the Lion's Den**
Seemingly a unique depiction of this subject in the Bassanos' *oeuvre*.

BARTHOLOMEUS BREENBERGH (c.1598–1657)
*Classical Ruins with Christ and the Woman of Canaan**
Signed and dated 1635
The ruins are based on the Forum in Rome, where Breenbergh stayed from 1619 to 1629. Again, the frame suggests it came from Murray's collection.

EAST WALL (INSET OVER FIREPLACE):

JAN WYCK (1640–1702)
A Battle-piece
Signed: *J Wijk*

Christian armies fighting the Turks. A topical subject, as it was apparently placed here only in 1683, the year of the relief of Vienna.

EAST WALL (INSET OVER DOOR):

HENRY DANCKERTS (c.1625–c.1679)
The Gardens at Pratolino
Signed: *HD, 1673*
Shows Giambologna's *Appeninno* in the celebrated gardens of the Villa Pratolino near Florence, which were already falling into decay.

FURNITURE

The ebony pier-table and candlestands with caned tops, c.1675, are probably Dutch and were originally *en suite* with a caned pier-glass, described in 1679 as a 'great looking glasse with an ebony frame caned'.

The ebony pier-glass is probably Dutch, c.1675.

The ebony cabinet on stand is Dutch, c.1675, and is presumably the 'great black ebony Cabinet' that was moved here from the Long Gallery by 1683. Inside the doors (which have to be kept closed to avoid straining the hinges) there are numerous small drawers designed to store papers. This cabinet (together with the ebony pier-table and candlestands) may be 'the cabinet of black ebonie' which the Duchess bought in Holland in 1672.

On the ebony table, c.1675, is a *tic-tac turntable clock* with strike and alarm in an architectural case of olivewood and ebony by Thomas Tompion (1639–1713). Possibly made in 1683, it may be his earliest surviving spring clock and is apparently unique for its case of olivewood oyster veneer: most of Tompion's spring clocks are in ebony cases. The clock is kindly loaned by Mrs Butterworth. Under the ebony table is a *miniature cabinet* of European inlaid lacquerwork on a giltwood base of c.1820.

PORCELAIN

The Chinese blue-and-white porcelain, arranged *en masse* in seventeenth-century style, is Kangxi, c.1700 or slightly earlier.

THE DUCHESS'S BEDCHAMBER

In the 1650s this was the nursery, where Elizabeth Dysart's eleven children by her first husband were brought up. In 1672 it was described as 'My Lady's Alcove roome', but by 1673 she had ceded it to her second husband. By 1677 the Duchess was again in occupation, and the Duke moved to the Volury Room.

The symmetrical composition of the alcove, its surround carved in 1673 with 'great rafle leaves', appears to be based on Jean le Pautre's 1660s engravings. The bed (already replaced by 1728) and the wall-hangings are modern interpretations of their 1679 predecessors of 'Morella Mohayre Scarlet & Black with embroidered borders wth. black & blew tufted fringe'. Unfortunately, by comparison with surviving embroidered textiles of this date (in the Queen's Antechamber and the Museum Room), the rich complexity of the damask, embroidery and

The walnut strong-box, c.1675, in the Duchess's Bedchamber

passementerie (trimmings) has not been achieved. Textiles, as the Duchess's bills show, were highly expensive, intended to convey a sense of conspicuous consumption. The expense and difficulty of achieving the required effect, together with the survival of the 1730s bed that succeeded the Duchess's in the alcove (see p.39), suggest the logic of returning to the 4th Earl's arrangement of the room in the 1730s and 1740s. This will be carried out in due course.

PICTURES

INSET OVER DOORS:

WILLIAM VAN DE VELDE The Younger (1633–1707)
Four Sea-pieces
All signed and dated 1673, a year after the father and the son left Amsterdam to seek work in England. Here by 1673. Having been painted before the Duke relinquished this room, they have distinctly masculine connotations.

INSET OVER WEST DOOR:

Calm: A Kaag near the Shore with other Vessels

INSET OVER DOOR TO LEFT OF ALCOVE:

Storm: Two English ships being driven ashore on to Rocks

INSET OVER DOOR TO RIGHT OF ALCOVE:

Calm: An English Frigate at anchor firing a Salute

INSET OVER EAST DOOR:

Storm: An English Galliot beating to Windward in a Gale

OVER FIREPLACE:

Sir PETER LELY (1618–80)
Elizabeth Murray, Lady Tollemache, later Countess of Dysart and Duchess of Lauderdale (1626–98)
Probably painted in or before 1648, the year of her marriage to Sir Lionel Tollemache.

CEILING OF ALCOVE:

Style of ANTONIO VERRIO (c.1639–1707)
Flora attended by Cupids

FURNITURE

The walnut strong-box mounted in brass, c.1675, on a gilded stand c.1730 may be one of two 'strong boxes' listed here in 1683.

The strong-box on a stand veneered in kingwood, c.1675, is probably German or Flemish, and must be the 'box with an extraordinary Lock' listed here in 1683. The curious locking device involves numerous hasps which secure the lid to the frame

The black and gilt chairs are similar to the 'thre arm'd Chairs carved & black & gilded' here in 1679, and are from a long set, some of which may be reproductions, of *c.*1813.

The fire-screen, c.1675, in the form of an iron tripod with silver mounts, is probably the 'Screen with a Screen Stick garnished wth Silver' in the 1683 inventory, although the tapestry panel is probably eighteenth-century and may have been added by William Bradshaw in 1736.

IN WINDOW BAY:

On the *marquetry table, c.1675*, is a folding mirror designed both for use on a table or on the wall. Its silver mounts are probably Dutch and the ripple-moulded ebony frame is consistent with a Dutch origin. It may have been part of the set of ebony and silver furniture listed here in 1677, and was possibly the 'splendid mirror framed in massive silver' that Augustus Hare saw here *c.*1880 on a 'hideous rough deal scullery table' (see p.75).

PORCELAIN

ON CHIMNEY:

The blue-and-white jar and cover and the bowl are Kangxi (1662–1722); *the lobed vase* is Ming (late sixteenth-century).

THE DUKE'S CLOSET

Completed in 1674, this was the most private of the Duke's apartments, though by 1677 he had relinquished the adjoining bedchamber to the Duchess. It was designed for warmth: 'panes to double ye sashes of my Lord's clositt' were installed in 1674 and there was a *portière* (a pair of curtains) inside the door, hung from a 'guilt Curtaine rod'. A 'Sleeping Chayre' (now at Helmingham) stood opposite the door beneath a curtained canopy decorated with 'silk strings with tassells'.

The upholstery was *en suite* with the wall-hangings 'of black and olive colloured Damask hangings wt a scarlet fringe wt silver & black edging'. The present hangings are modern interpretations of *c.*1970.

PICTURES

INSET OVER CHIMNEYPIECE:

THOMAS WYCK (1616–77)
An Alchemist
Signed: *T. Wijk*
Here by 1679.

INSET OVER FIREPLACE:

WILLIAM VAN DE VELDE the Younger
(1633–1707)
A Sea Battle
Here by 1679.

INSET OVER DOOR:

THOMAS WYCK (1616–77)
A View of the Forum
Signed: *T. Wijk*
Here by 1679.

CEILING:

Style of ANTONIO VERRIO (*c.*1639–1707)
Two Female Figures representing Musical Harmony, with Cupids scattering Flowers

COVE:

Cupids tying up Garlands

FURNITURE

The writing-cabinet veneered in walnut, burr elm and ebony, *c.*1675, has traces of silvering on the legs, which, with its silver mounts, would have complemented the silvered couch and pair of chairs that stood here in 1677, when it was described as a 'Scritore done with Silver'. In 1731 George Nix supplied '4 new black Balls' (or feet) in the course of repairs.

The armchair of walnut with partial gilding is *c.*1675.

PORCELAIN

The blue-and-white china is Kangxi, with the exception of the Delft bottle vase on the stretcher of the writing-cabinet.

The visitor should leave the Duchess's Bedchamber by the door to the right of the bed alcove and cross the West Passage.

THE STEWARD'S HALL

The Steward's Hall and Back Parlour were for the use of the senior domestic staff, classed as 'gentlemen' in the Lauderdale inventories. Some may have been of gentle birth – young men attached to the ducal household in order to polish their manners, and who provided a degree of service in return. A second-floor bedroom was designated 'The Gentlemen's Chamber'. The steward was the head of the household staff and, as at Uppark and Petworth in Sussex, was supported by a butler (mentioned in the 1728 inventory, and *en poste* in 1655, though not apparently in the Lauderdale period) and a housekeeper, who had responsibility for the male and female servants respectively. The first room was the dining-room, where in 1677 the steward, seated on a separate chair, presided over a long cedarwood table with two benches on either side. There was also an 'oyster table' in 1677, a reminder that oysters were then common fare.

PICTURES

SOUTH WALL:

After Sir ANTHONY VAN DYCK (1599–1641)
Charles I (1600–49) on Horseback
A later reduced copy of the most famous equestrian portrait of the King, now in the National Gallery.

WEST WALL:

? ITALIAN, c.1600
Fra Paolo Sarpi (1552–1623)*
Inscribed: CONCILII TRIDENTINI EVISCERATOR
A highly critical Venetian historian of the Council of Trent (1545–63), so much admired by Protestants.

NORTH WALL:

ENGLISH, late seventeenth-century
Supposed portrait of Ralph Wilbraham of Newbottle
Younger son of Sir Thomas Wilbraham, 2nd Bt (c.1601–60), of Woodhey. His niece, Grace, married the 3rd Earl of Dysart in 1680. But since he was born c.1630–5, he cannot be the sitter here.

Manner of Sir PETER LELY (1618–80)
Sir Thomas Delves, Bt (1630–1713)
Grandson of Sir Roger Wilbraham, Master of Requests to James I. Wilbraham's great-granddaughter, Grace Wilbraham, married the 3rd Earl of Dysart.

? ENGLISH, c.1750
? *Lionel, 5th Earl of Dysart (1734–99)*
If of him, painted as a young man, when still Viscount Huntingtower. After inheriting the Dysart and Tollemache estates in 1770, he refused to make any changes or repairs at Ham, and demolished two of the secondary Tollemache seats: Harrington Hall, Northamptonshire (inherited from the Stanhopes) and Woodhey, Cheshire (inherited from the Wilbrahams).

EAST WALL:

Attributed to PHILIP WICKSTEAD (active 1763–c.1790)
Group of Gentlemen on the Grand Tour, c.1773
From left to right: John Corbett, the Hon. John Tollemache (third son of the 4th Earl of Dysart), John Chetwynd-Talbot (created Earl Talbot 1784), James Byres (Scottish antiquarian and art dealer resident in Rome), Sir John Rous, John Staples and William McDowall.

SOUTH WALL (OVER DOOR):

ENGLISH, late seventeenth-century
A Child at a Fountain
Possibly a member of the Thynne family.

THE BACK PARLOUR

This inner room was mainly for relaxation. There were three oval 'tables of Wainescot' (ie of oak to match the fitted cupboards) and twelve chairs covered in 'turkie work', subsequently replaced by the same number of cedar tables and a set of caned chairs. There was a sideboard with a black marble wine-cooler beneath, which suggests that occasionally this larger room was also used for dining. By 1683 there was also a 'scriptore of walnutree' for writing. The walls were hung with tapestry (in 1677) and there were 'red Serge window Curtaines', so this was a well-appointed room, designed to enhance the status of its occupants.

In 1728 the 'Stewards Parlour' still contained its 'Old' seventeenth-century contents, but by 1844 it had become the 'Housekeeper's Room' comfortably furnished with 'A Brussels carpet plan'd to room', and mahogany furniture including a dining-table, dumb waiter and even a card-table. By 1911 it was a masculine 'Smoking Room'. From 1844 the outer room was simply an ante-room with no specific purpose.

PICTURES

CLOCKWISE, FROM BESIDE DOOR:

Manner of GERRIT VAN HONTHORST (1590–1656)
Charles Maitland, Lord Halton, 3rd Earl of Lauderdale (1620–91)
Brother and political collaborator of the Duke of Lauderdale. When the Duke died in 1682, he left the majority of his Scottish estates (including the ancient seat of the Maitland family) to the Duchess, who maintained that his brother should pay his English debts and funeral expenses. The new Earl not surprisingly contested the will in court, and spent many years in costly litigation with the unrepentant Duchess. This and the two other pictures in the manner of Honthorst make a set, which would appear to indicate that the sitters were in Holland in 1653.

Manner of GERRIT VAN HONTHORST (1590–1656)
? Jane Lauder, Lady Elphinstone
Dated 1653, so this may represent Elizabeth Lauder's elder sister who married Sir Thomas Elphinstone of Calder Hall, but for some reason did not inherit her parents' estates.

Attributed to JOAN CARLILE (1606?–79)
Elizabeth Murray, Countess of Dysart (1626–98), with her first husband, Sir Lionel Tollemache (1624–69), and her sister, Lady Maynard (c.1638–82)
Joan Carlile lived close to Ham at Petersham Lodge, Richmond Park. Her husband, the playwright Lodowick Carlile, had been appointed Keeper of the Park by Charles I. The Carliles appear to have been close friends of the Murrays (Lodowick had dedicated his first play to William Murray), and

were staunch Royalists during the Civil War. Painted after 1648, the year of Elizabeth's marriage to Sir Lionel, and an unusually early example of a conversation piece in England.

Manner of GERRIT VAN HONTHORST (1590–1656)
? Elizabeth Lauder, Countess of Lauderdale (d.1685–91)
Pendant to the portrait of the Earl of Lauderdale (above), and so probably his wife (they married in 1653). She was the younger daughter, co-heir and inheritrix of the estates of Richard Lauder (d. after 1660) and his wife, Mary or Mariota Scot, Lady Haltoun, or Halton. These included Halton Hall, from which Maitland took his title as Lord of Session (1670–82).

SOUTH WALL (OVER DOOR):

Manner of JAN WYCK (1640–1702)
A Battle Scene
Bought by the 4th Earl of Dysart at Lord Cholmondeley's sale in 1748 for £1 10s, as by Tillemans.

FURNITURE

The set of four armchairs is English, c.1760, of mahogany covered in a three-colour woollen velvet of the type known as caffoy.

THE WEST PASSAGE

In 1638 the wainscot was 'thrise coullored over with Amber in Oylle, and then with light Timber collor' to give the effect of wood graining. The earliest colour on the present panelling (renewed in 1673) is a pale grey. A more modern (probably nineteenth-century) scheme has been repeated in the recent redecoration.

The Lauderdale inventories list 'one long Matt' on the floor, a cupboard (made in 1674 'for botelles and plates') and a 'chain'd wainscot table', which may have been an oak gate-leg dining-table stored here when not in use. There were 'Two glass Lanthornes', which may be the ones still *in situ*, and a clock, perhaps the regulator longcase clock in a plain oak case by Joseph Knibb (1640–1711) now in a private collection. Knibb charged in 1673 for 'takeing down ye great Repeating Clock at Whitehall [the Lauderdales' lodging in the Palace] and setting it up againe at Ham'. This would have been the clock by which the household monitored the daily routine and by which the other clocks (including others by Knibb) were set.

The leather fire buckets are possibly seventeenth-century.

PICTURES

FLEMISH, mid-seventeenth-century
A Hound
Evidently a fragment from a whole-length portrait of a sportsman.

Attributed to SIMON VAN DER DOES (1653–1718)
A Goat and a Ram

SCULPTURE

OVER DOOR:

ALEXANDER MACDONALD (b.1847)
William Tollemache, 9th Earl of Dysart (1859–1935)
White marble; signed and dated: *Rome 1879*
The 9th Earl renovated Ham in the 1890s.

The visitor walks back towards the Great Hall and turns left into the Buttery.

THE BUTTERY

A strategically placed servery between the Kitchen and offices below stairs, and the rooms used for dining and entertaining, this is where the food and drink would have been laid out and checked by the butler before being served.

The panelling dates from the building of the house: in 1638, it was 'thrise prymmed over, and layde greene in Oylle'. Then, and in the Lauderdale period, the Buttery contained practical furniture: in 1683 a 'Counter', 'two paire of large tables', 'one bin for bread and Linnen', 'one Cupboard for glasses', and baskets for carrying glasses, plates and bread to the table. There was also a 'Cupboard for glasses', a 'presse for Linnen', a 'water bucket', 'Two Leather Chayres' and a 'Japan voyder' (possibly the painted tray still in the house) for gathering up crumbs from the dining-tables.

In 1638 and thereafter the Buttery also contained 'A great cupboard for the plate [silver]' and in 1683 'Two travelling Chests for plate' (essential equipment for the ducal peregrinations between Scotland, Whitehall and Ham). The butler was also responsible for the security of the silver. His adjoining bedroom ('The buttery Chamber') contained another 'chest for plate'.

METALWORK

The copper wine-cooler, c.1675, is probably the 'Copper Basket' listed in 1683.

The visitor descends the stairs to the Basement.

THE BASEMENT

Below stairs were 'The lower Offices' as they were called in 1683. These were extensive, although it is not always possible to locate precisely the rooms that are referred to in the Lauderdale inventories. They included the Kitchen, Scullery and Servants' Hall (in 1677, the 'Usher of the Hall' had his own office), as well as a laundry, pantries and larders. These last included a 'wet Larder', a 'Still House' (containing 'Three stills with pewter heads' for distilling fruit, flower and medicinal waters), and 'Cellers' containing wine, brewing equipment, barrels of beer and even 'One Deale Chest for faule Linnen'.

The Basement was where the servants worked, relaxed and ate. They slept in garrets on the top storey, although the steward, housekeeper, 'Clerke of the Kitchin' and cook all had separate bedrooms, befitting their superior status (as did the Duke's 'Gentleman of the Horse' and chaplain). The back stairs gave access to their own quarters and to the family's private apartments. When the Lauderdales were in residence, the basement would have been a hive of activity, especially, as in 1672, 'when ye King dyn'd here'. When the Duke and Duchess were away, as in the winter, a skeleton staff would have remained behind as caretakers.

It would appear from the inventories that the 'Wash house', 'Bakhouse' (for baking bread, etc.), 'Still House' and 'Dayry' were also downstairs, though one would expect them to have been in the yard outside. Certainly, there was a secondary laundry outside in 1677, and the 'Bakehouses' were re-roofed in 1672, although there was a smaller 'baking roome' in the basement. The domestic offices and ancilliary buildings such as the Brewhouse were completely renovated between 1672 and 1674, the tradesmen's bills indicating compre-

The Kitchen

The Basement rooms are in course of rearrangement pending further research into their history and function.

hensive improvements to the structure and equipment of each department. They also show that the house depended upon its own small agricultural estate, including a cow-yard, wood-yard, pigsty, hen-house, a granary and ranges of barns, as well as saddle, carriage and cart-horse stables. This was still the case in 1844, although by then, 'most of the farm implements [were] laid aside as worn and useless'.

The domestic offices remained much the same in the subsequent centuries. By 1911 the 'Upper Servants' Dining Room', the Housekeeper's Room and even the 'Butler's Bed Sitting Room' were all in the basement, and so it remained until at least 1935, the distinctions between grades of staff in a large household persisting well into the twentieth century.

THE KITCHEN AND PANTRY

The Kitchen almost certainly occupies its original site, and, with the Scullery and other offices, was brought up to date in 1672. For example, the 'Kytching chimney' was rebuilt, and the 'sinck in ye Kitchin' was remade, and the floor and the drains were repaired. The Kitchen was of course the cook's domain, but at Ham there was also a Clerk of the Kitchen, who would have ordered the provisions and kept the accounts.

There was a large amount of equipment, which included (in 1677) nine spits (four were for grilling larks), numerous pots, pans and kettles with 'trevatts' (trivets) to put them on, pans for baking pies, 'two Cullenders', 'one tosting irone', three cleavers and a 'flesh fork'. There was a 'pestle and Morter' (on view) and a flour box. The 1683 inventory listed a 'Jack with three Chaines' to drive the spits, gridirons for grilling and roasting, 'Stewing dishes', 'tart pans', 'one Carp pan and cover', 'one tin dredging box', a spice box and an 'apple roaster of tin'. There were also pewter plates and 'Two pewter salts'.

Ham was self-sufficient in milk, eggs, butter, bread, vegetables, poultry, pork and beef. Baking, making preserves, distilling and brewing beer were done on the premises. The household records between 1668 and 1677 reveal that there were also large accounts with specialist suppliers: the butcher, fishmonger, poulterer, baker, grocer and vintner are all mentioned. The bills show that large amounts of vegetables, fruit and fish were consumed as well as meat. The prices naturally varied according to the season and to quality (lemons fluctuated between 1s and 3s per dozen; cherries between $1\frac{1}{2}$d and 5s per pound; butter cost 4d to 8d a pound – ordinary, fresh, salt and sweet were available). Seafood and fish were plentiful: oysters, prawns, crabs, crayfish, sole, whiting, cod, lampreys, eels, perch, gudgeon, carp, trout, salmon and turbot were all ordered regularly. Game included pheasants, woodcock, teal, quail and larks (which were eaten in December, January and February and cost 6s for five dozen).

In 1728 the Kitchen inventory was much the same, but by 1844 'a very stout kitchen range with full bar spit racks and swing trivets' had been installed. The 'deal dresser with 7 drawers, a pot board and 3 shelves over as fixed' and the 'dresser as fixed at the end of the room with cupboards under enclosed by folding doors' are still *in situ*. In 1911 the Kitchen contained 'the usual kitchen furniture etc. with utensils, crockery and glass'. The 1947 cast-iron range was removed *c.*1980, when the Kitchen and the adjoining 'Larder within ye Kitching', as it was called in 1677, were restored in seventeenth-century style.

FURNITURE

The kitchen table is a venerable object, which may well be seventeenth-century.

ON DRESSER:

Much of the stoneware and other useful ceramics are kindly loaned by the Museum of London.

THE SERVANTS' HALL

Subsequently tiled and provided with shelving, this was probably the site of the seventeenth-century hall where the servants dined and enjoyed what little relaxation they could. In 1683 its furnishings were spartan: 'Two deale tables, Two deale forms, One old Cupboarde, One deale Presse, One Settle Bed, Two large Copper pots lin'd, One smaller copper lin'd'. In 1728 the picture was similar, although the furniture seems to have been replaced by 'A long Cedar table; a Cedar Form; a Cupboard and benches round'. In 1911 the servants still sat on forms at a long table, but there were a few Windsor chairs and a pair of oak settles that were probably placed either side of the fire.

THE DUCHESS'S BATHROOM

This was 'The Bathing Roome' of the Duchess of Lauderdale listed within her apartment from 1677, and linked by a staircase to her bedroom above via the 'Gentlewoman's Chamber'. The 'bathing tubb and little stoole within it' was probably placed in the smaller room still paved in black and white. A tent-like canopy was arranged around the bath creating a steamy atmosphere within, rather like a Turkish bath. Afterwards, the Duchess would have retired to the main room (warmed by a fireplace) which contained:

One painted Bedstead, two quiltes and a bolster
Four curtaines of painted Satten wth three Curtaine rods, tester and head Cloath of wte Satten, counterpane of ye same.

Here she could rest, anointed with oil and enveloped in towels. There were four chairs, one upholstered *en suite* with the bed.

It is often thought that little attention was paid to bathing in the seventeenth century, but at Ham there was also a bathhouse in the yard, presumably for the use of the household. The Duchess's Bathroom continued in use (despite its distance from the upper floors) and was fitted by the 9th Earl with the latest in early twentieth-century multiple-jet showers, positioned here perhaps to obtain the maximum water pressure, the tank being in the attic.

Visitors leave the house by the side door.

CHAPTER TWO
TOUR OF THE GARDEN

After dinner I walked to Ham to see the House and Garden of the Duke of Lauderdale, which is indeed inferior to few of the best Villas in Italy itself; the House furnished like a great Prince's; the Parterres, Flower Gardens, Orangeries, Groves, Avenues, Courts, Statues, Perspectives, Fountains, Aviaries and all this at the banks of the Sweetest River in the World, must needs be surprising.

John Evelyn's description, written in 1678, evokes the splendour of the gardens at Ham at the end of a decade of prodigious expenditure by the Lauderdales. The restoration of the east and south compartments of the garden in 1975 began the process of re-establishing this layout. Work remains to be done to return more of the elaborate features admired by Evelyn, and the National Trust hopes that this will help visitors understand and enjoy the gardens as they appeared in their heyday.

Sir Thomas Vavasour surrounded his new house with an elaborate formal garden. Robert Smythson's drawing of 1609 (illustrated opposite) shows a series of sunken concentric parterres laid out around a central oval on axis with the south front of the house. This garden could be viewed from the raised gravel walkways that surrounded it. An orchard and vegetable garden are also shown to the south of the house. The plan was novel for England and may have been based on Claude Mollet I's garden at St Germain-en-Laye, made for Henri IV in 1599–1610. However, it is unlikely that the Ham scheme was executed exactly as shown by Smythson. Recent archaeological investigation has also cast doubt on the reliability of his drawing.

Although little evidence has been found for William Murray's work in the garden, his improvements may have been quite substantial. A large bill drawn up in 1633 (Tollemache MSS 116, Grantham) describes in elaborate terms how a length of wall was built by a Roberto Palmere.

The second marriage of Elizabeth, Countess of Dysart to John Maitland, Earl of Lauderdale in 1672 began a period of ambitious alterations and extentions to the grounds. No doubt the Lauderdales were building on the improvements made by Elizabeth's father, and we know that Lauderdale was involved with Lady Dysart's alterations to Ham in 1670, before their marriage. Apart from the building accounts and correspondence (which are considerable), our knowledge of the appearance of the late seventeenth-century garden derives from inventories, lists and descriptions, and from views and plans (some are on display in the house).

The 1679 inventory lists the contents of various parts of the garden. Also important are the inventory of the Duke's goods and chattels, drawn up after his death in 1682; a list of trees and plants for the garden, again of about 1682; and, lastly, an 'Account of ye trees, plants, flowers and potts, su[ch] were delivered to Jno Balesson Yo[r] Graces Gardner ab[t] y[e] Midle of June 1693'. Although the differences between the lists of 1682 and 1693 are not as great as might be expected, given the financial difficulties of the Duchess after her husband's death, the former probably provides a more accurate impression of the garden at its height in the 1670s.

The key document is John Slezer and Jan Wyck's survey plan of the garden of c.1671–2 (illustrated on p.54). The Scottish architect Sir William Bruce, who may have redesigned the house for the Lauderdales (see p.64), was probably also consulted about alterations to the garden and indeed may have been partly responsible for the Slezer and Wyck design. Under Bruce's direction, Slezer and Wyck had already surveyed other Lauderdale properties in Scotland, and elements of their garden design for Lethington show striking similarities to the layout recorded for Ham. This may be evidence for a repetitive taste in gardening or perhaps, alternatively, a schematic approach by the artist for drawing a garden layout. The design for Ham shows the area of the orchard and vegetable garden (as described on the Smythson drawing) now incorporated into the south garden, which consisted of eight grass plats and extended to a 'wilderness'. The North Forecourt was also extended to the north and the stable yard to the east. To the west the drawing shows a large garden consisting of 32 compartments with an orangery at its northern end. The garden to the east is described in the 1679 inventory as the Cherry Garden and is the successor to the 'Principall' garden of Smythson's layout. Axial avenue planting and a closely planted tree layout to the east of the Cherry Garden, extending to the full length of the garden, are also recorded on

the drawing. The various features of the grounds in the 1670s will be described at the relevant point of the garden tour below.

The period between 1682 and 1727 saw little activity, as the estate was left encumbered by debts after the extravagancies of the 1670s. A structural survey of the house was carried out for the 4th Earl in 1730, and a layout drawing of the grounds (collection Lord Tollemache, Helmingham) may be related to this survey. In painstaking and accurate detail, this plan shows the appearance of the garden before 1740. Architectural changes made to the façade of the house after that date are recorded in outline on the drawing. The Cherry Garden appears as a single large square of grass; the Orchard has a pond in the centre. However, the engraving in

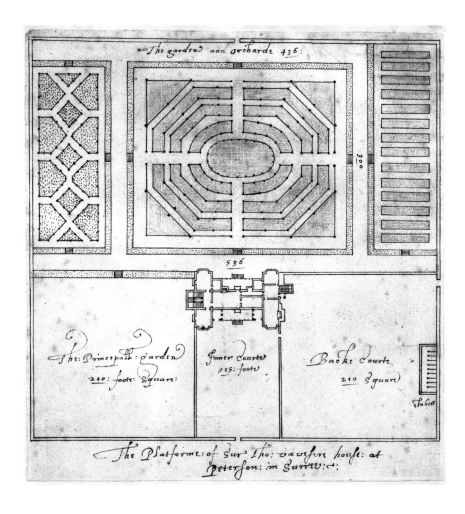

Robert Smythson's plan of Ham, c.1609 (British Architectural Library, RIBA)

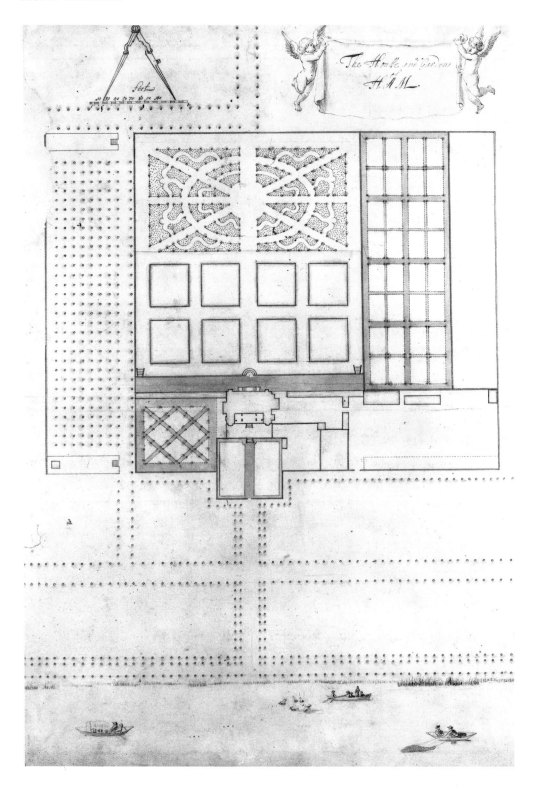

The House and Garden
H.M.

Vitruvius Britannicus (1739) shows variations to the layout from the earlier drawings, which demonstrates that there are some gaps in our knowledge of the garden's development, and the need for caution in interpreting such evidence.

Both the 3rd and 4th Earls maintained the garden, and retained the essentials of the seventeenth-century layout. In 1742, for example, 'Wright, Gardener' was paid £120 a year, and in 1745 'Griffin, ye gardener' was paid for 'putting ye gardens in order'. In 1743 '2 barge loads of ashes for ye gardens' were delivered. In 1752 the 4th Earl made an arrangement with another gardener, George Long, who was to receive a £100 salary:

to keep ye Pleasure Ground in a handsome manner and to stock my kitchen ground with plenty of every thing necessary, he is not to have ye liberty of selling ye produce of ye gardens. I am to find a horse to roll, Orange Trees, melon lights and frames, and supply ye fruit trees. He is to find Dung.

Orange trees continued to be an important element in what was still a formally arranged garden. In 1758 five men were paid 'for trenching ye Wilderness Garden, grubbing up trees etc'. In 1763 138 elms were planted, and 500 more were 'planted in and about Ham walks'. These latter payments may suggest a deformalisation of the garden, and certainly by *c.*1780, when a series of watercolours was painted for the 5th Earl (collection Lord Tollemache), the seventeenth-century parterres on the south front had been replaced by a large lawn with clumps of trees and shrubs in the style of 'Capability' Brown.

The 5th Earl's brother, Wilbraham, who inherited the title in 1799, altered the North Forecourt, installing the Coade stone *River God*. The Cherry Garden and present Orangery Garden were altered further in the nineteenth century, when elaborate herbaceous borders were laid out along the north front of the house. Most of this Victorian work has now disappeared. At the turn of the century the North Forecourt railings were installed, replacing the dwarf wall seen in the watercolours by Thomas Rowlandson. During the Second World War the garden was damaged by bombing and ran

(Left)
Plan of the garden, c.1671–2; attributed to John Slezer and Jan Wyck (Library Closet)

(Right)
Bird's-eye view of Ham from the south; engraving from 'Vitruvius Britannicus' (1739)

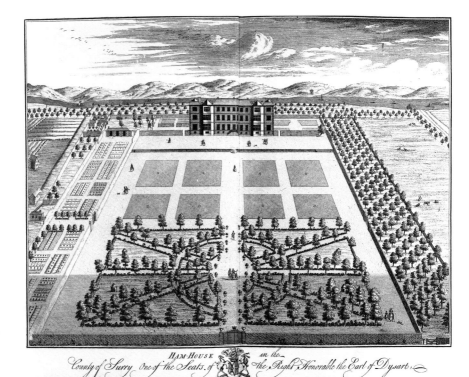

Lord Dysart treating his Tenantry; by Thomas Rowlandson, 1803 (collection the Hon. Michael Tollemache)

to seed. When the house came to the National Trust in 1948, the worst of the wartime damage was repaired, but otherwise the garden remained largely unaltered until 1975. In that year a large private donation allowed the garden to be restored in part to a seventeenth-century layout, as one of the Trust's contributions to European Architectural Heritage Year. The principal alterations were to re-create the Wilderness, to return the eight plats to the south and to re-create the Cherry Garden. The Slezer and Wyck plan was used as the primary visual source to guide the restoration. The National Trust hopes to embark upon the second stage of the restoration in the late 1990s.

THE NORTH MEADOW

There have always been wooden fences around the North Meadow, but originally (and certainly in the Lauderdale period) these were painted (as is still the custom on Ham Common). An avenue leads from the house to the river, an important artery of communication in the seventeenth century, when the roads were poor. The Duke and Duchess, as well as important visitors such as the King, would have alighted from their barges at the landing place, from where the Twickenham ferry has operated since Charles II's reign. Here too were off-loaded materials for the house, from 'Scotch marble' for chimneypieces to silk and furniture imported from France and Holland.

The Slezer and Wyck plan shows a single line of trees parallel to the riverbank, a double planting beyond, and along the avenue another line of trees. Unfortunately, the regularity of the intended effect has been lost somewhat. The probably pre-1740 plan shows a half-circle of trees and a series of steps at the river end, providing an impressive approach to the house from the riverbank. John Rocque's survey of this area of Surrey records a network of avenues, aligned and uniformly planted throughout the area, providing grand vistas and a sense of order. A programme of replanting and restoration is being undertaken over the next century by Richmond Borough Council, in co-operation with the National Trust and other owners of property in the area as part of the major project of improvements along the banks and hinterland of the Thames.

The Melancholy Walk was situated to the east of the Cherry Garden. Although the visual evidence for the detailed planting of this area is inconsistent, the reason why this compartment was created is usefully summarised by Ralph Thoresby in 1712: 'Ham. We walked through the delicate meadows near the river, and trees artfully planted in the quincunx order making agreeable views and walks in different ways'. Viewing platforms were built at either end of the Melancholy Walk; that to the north was also provided with a banqueting house. A mason's bill for July and August 1672 refers to 'working and setting 2 stories in ye banquetting house', and repairs were carried out in 1752 and 1753. Such a feature again confirms that Ham was in the vanguard of fashion, as described in John Worlidge's *Systema Horticulturea* (1677):

It is not unusual to raise a Mount with the wast Earth or rubbish, you may otherwise happen to be troubled withal at some convenient distance for your house on which as on your Terrace walks you have the advantage of the air and prospect, and whereon you may erect a Pleasure or Banqueting house, or such like place of repose.

Alas, the building at Ham was destroyed.

The Cherry Garden

THE CHERRY GARDEN

The inventories and surviving drawings for the Cherry Garden suggest that it was intended to display the most costly and intricate effects, relying on choice shrubs and flowers in beds and elaborate vases. The 1679 inventory lists:

One Marble statue upon a stone pedestall
Twelve flower pots of stone upon stone pedestalls
Tenn flower pots of lead guilt
Tenn wooden stooles with benches painted

It is likely that the cherry trees which gave the garden its name were planted against the walls. Recent archaeological investigation has revealed the retaining wall of the terrace along the south side of the garden. This led directly from the White Closet to the *clairvoyée* which provided a view into the Melancholy Walk. The gilded lead and stone vases were probably placed along the terrace and flower border which was by the terrace. By 1786 the south wall and possibly also the north walls of the garden were demolished.

The 1975 restoration relied on the Slezer and Wyck drawings to create the present layout at the centre of the garden. It was realised with dwarf box and clipped box cones, with alternating santolina and lavender in the centre of each box hedge compartment. Two *berceaux* (vaulted trellises) of pleached hornbeam were also created. The statue of *Bacchus*, which is the only free-standing sculpture to survive from the Lauderdales' garden, will be placed in the centre.

THE SOUTH TERRACE AND PLATS

Because of its scale, the series of eight plats created by the Lauderdales to the south of the house was possibly the most dramatic of their alterations to the garden. The restoration of this area in the 1970s was a considerable achievement, reversing the change which had occurred in the later eighteenth century, when the plats were replaced by a single sweep of lawn. On the terrace wall the numerous shallow platforms were the bases for the vases which decorated the terrace and which are seen in the drawing of the south front attributed to Slezer (illustrated on p.67). No doubt on the terrace and

alongside the plats were located many of the 42 boxes containing large orange and lemon trees, myrtles, oleander and pomegranate mentioned in the list of *c*.1682. Also 327 pots are listed, no doubt of varying sizes depending on the maturity of the trees or flowers within.

A number of sources, visual and documentary, suggest that sculpture decorated the centre of each plat. Painters' bills for 1673 and 1674 and the 1679 inventory refer to '10 statues of lead, whereof two upon stone pedestals, and 8 upon wooden pedestalls'. Lead was probably the most usual material for garden statues in the 1660s, although scarcely any survive. We know that the Lauderdales imported nine statues from Holland to Edinburgh in 1675.

THE WILDERNESS

The garden to the south of the plats is the Wilderness, laid out in grass walks as a *patte d'oie* (goose's foot) in sixteen compartments of hornbeam hedges and field maple. Henry Danckerts's painting of the south front from the Wilderness (illustrated on p.59) gives an excellent idea of what was intended. The Trust has attempted to return most of the elements (with the exception of the statues) seen in the painting of the central clearing of the Wilderness. The sculptures which can be identified in Danckerts's painting are copies of Giambologna's *Mercury* and *Fortuna*, as well as the celebrated Antique *Venus de' Medici*. They appear to have been painted to simulate bronze. The four summer-houses reproduce those seen in the *Vitruvius Britannicus* engraving. On the overthrow to the south gates are the Tollemache coat of arms quartered with those of Murray, and the motto of the Order of the Thistle, *Nemo Me Impune Lacessit* ('No man can harm me with impunity'). The ironwork on this gate and elsewhere at Ham is painted in a version of Smalt blue, used in the seventeenth century.

The south front from the Wilderness, c.1675–9; attributed to Henry Danckerts (White Closet)

THE ORANGERY GARDEN

Passing through the gateway in the west wall, with its recently reproduced gate copying its partner in the east wall opposite, visitors reach the Ilex Walk, at the south end of the Orangery Garden. This garden appears in all the drawings with numerous compartments for whose further interpretation future archaeology is needed. A cutting border supplying appropriate flowers for the house will be established along the east wall of the garden.

The northern end is dominated by the Orangery, which looks over what was once the Vegetable Garden. It was probably built for the Lauderdales between 1672 and 1674, but could be older. Orangeries were generally narrow buildings containing one large room heated by stoves, and lit by windows in the south wall. They played an important role in overwintering tender species intended for summer display. At the far end of the Ham building (in the present self-service area), there was also accommodation for gardeners. The Orangery

has been converted to a tea-room with little effect on its external appearance. Inside are displayed nineteenth-century casts after the Antique.

The stable block behind the Orangery and facing Ham Street dates from the seventeenth century, but was altered and extended in 1787 (and is in private ownership).

THE WEST COURTYARD AND ORCHARD

The circuit concludes with the West Courtyard and beyond, the Orchard Garden. The ice-house between these areas was built c.1800 and has a fine domed brick interior. In the era before mechanical refrigeration, ice was stored in a pit packed in straw, and brought in to the house during the summer when needed. The exterior was covered with concrete during the Second World War so that it could be used as an air-raid shelter. Archaeological investigation of the Orchard has revealed the central pond seen in the pre-1740 plan, and in time it is hoped to reinstate this feature.

CHAPTER THREE

THE 1ST EARL AND COUNTESS OF DYSART

Ham House was built for Sir Thomas Vavasour in 1610, when the date and the loyal inscription 'Vivat Rex' were carved on the front door. Sir Thomas came from an ancient Yorkshire family, and had been a colourful figure at the Elizabethan court. A regular competitor in the royal tilts, he was also a valiant naval captain during the war against Spain. In 1591 Vavasour's ship, the *Foresight*, was one of six warships anchored off the Azores when the Spanish attacked. He survived, but the *Revenge*, under the command of Richard Grenville, was sunk with all hands. Many raiding expeditions followed, and Vavasour was knighted at sea by Elizabeth's favourite, Essex, in 1597.

On the accession of James I in 1603, Sir Thomas was rewarded for his service with the rank of Knight Marshal, and several grants of land. He must have begun to build his new house at Ham in at least 1608, as the almost completed house and garden were drawn in detail by Robert Smythson in the summer of 1609. Smythson's plan of the original house (illustrated on p.53) shows a typical Jacobean H-plan, with the main entrance placed in the centre of the north front. Within, however, symmetry was ignored: the door led into one corner of the Great Hall in the traditional medieval way, although by this date the old screens passage had been abandoned. The entrance front has undergone only slight alterations since Vavasour's day; a miniature of 1649 shows a frontispiece or projecting bay above the front door, and turrets with ogee caps rising from the cloisters on either side. Inside the house, a number of features (mainly chimneypieces and panelling) remain from this period. Outside, archaeology has revealed traces of Vavasour's elaborate formal garden (see p.52).

Vavasour died in 1620, and the lease of Ham House passed to one of the King's favourites, John Ramsay, 1st Earl of Holdernesse, who had helped to rescue James when the 3rd Earl of Gowrie attempted to assassinate him in 1600. Holdernesse died in 1626, and Ham became the home of another Scotsman, William Murray, a childhood friend of the new King, Charles I.

Murray came from a cadet branch of the Murrays of Tullibardine, ancestors of the Dukes of Atholl. Murray's father was the second of six sons, and had entered the church, ending his days as parson of Dysart in Fife. Fortunately for young William's future, one of his uncles, Thomas, achieved an early success in academic circles. Having followed King James south in 1603, Thomas Murray was appointed personal tutor to Prince Charles in 1605. Soon

The north front appears in this 1649 miniature of Katherine Bruce, who married William Murray

afterwards his nephew William was asked to join the Prince's lessons as page and 'whipping boy', who was punished for the Prince's misdemeanours.

Murray grew up to become one of Charles's inner circle: in 1623 he accompanied Charles and Buckingham to Spain in the search for a royal bride, spending six months at the Spanish court. This was a golden opportunity for Charles and his friends to immerse themselves in the glories of the Spanish royal collection of Italian High Renaissance pictures. After his accession in 1625, Murray was appointed a Gentleman of the Bedchamber, and (according to Bishop Burnet) 'had great credit with him, not only in procuring private favours, but in all his counsels'. He was also at the centre of the 'Whitehall group' of collectors, connoisseurs and expert advisers which gathered around the King, a group that included Endymion Porter, Balthazar Gerbier and Inigo Jones.

In 1637 Charles granted Murray the lordship of the Manors of Ham and Petersham in recompense for the enclosure of part of his estate within Richmond Park. The increased income generated by this gift may have prompted Murray to re-decorate the interior of Ham House. From 1637 to 1639 he employed a group of master craftsmen, at least two of whom had worked for the crown, to bring Ham up to date with the latest French-inspired court fashions.

Murray's decorative schemes survive most completely in the sequence of first-floor State Rooms opening from the Great Stair he rebuilt: the Great Dining Room (now the Hall Gallery), North Drawing Room, Long Gallery and Green Closet. Intricately carved joinery was supplied by Thomas Carter, plasterwork by Joseph Kinsman and decorative paintwork by Matthew Goodricke. Franz Cleyn, principal designer for the Mortlake tapestry works, provided inset paintings for several of the rooms, and probably directed the overall project.

An inventory taken after Murray's death in 1655 shows that the house was fashionably appointed with co-ordinated colour schemes in which the wall-hangings, window-curtains, chair-coverings and table-covers all matched, producing a unified effect. Costly stamped and gilt leather was used in several rooms, and the window-curtains were even

William Murray, 1st Earl of Dysart; by David Paton

divided in two in the modern way – a startling innovation at that period. In Murray's day the family rooms were on the ground floor, with two main parlours filling the wings on either side of the Great Hall. On the floor above, two principal apartments (presumably those of Murray and his wife) led off the staircase landing, beyond which lay the suite of State Rooms. Subsidiary bedrooms filled the second floor, and servants were housed in the basement and attic.

That part of Murray's picture collection which survives at Ham provides striking evidence of his taste and knowledge. It comprises contemporary works by Italian and Flemish masters, copies of masterpieces by Titian and Correggio in the collections of Charles I and Philip IV of Spain, and several portraits, including a number of important miniatures by John Hoskins. The latter would have been housed in the ornate Green Closet, which we know held over 50 miniatures and small paintings by 1677. This tiny room forms the single surviving example of an English seventeenth-century 'miniature cabinet', inspired by that of Charles I at Whitehall.

The North Drawing Room, created for William Murray in 1637–9

Murray was to have little time to enjoy his redecorated house. Civil war broke out in 1642, and he naturally joined the King. 'Little Will Murray' became the trusted carrier of messages between Charles and his queen, Henrietta Maria, who had fled first to Holland, then to France. In 1643 Murray was ennobled for his services, being created Earl of Dysart and Viscount Huntingtower. For the next six years he continued to travel secretly between England, Scotland and the Continent, attempting to reach an agreement between Charles and the Scots. His activities were well known to Parliamentary agents; Robert Wright wrote from Paris in December 1645, 'The accorde so much desired betwixt the King and the Scots is with all diligence pursued by Mr Wm Murray, and the Queene is very confident

it will succeed'. Despite Murray's efforts, 'accorde' was never reached, and King Charles was executed in 1649. Murray then entered a more permanent exile in Holland, making occasional brief visits to Scotland. He died in Edinburgh in December 1655, when, following Scottish custom, the earldom passed to his eldest daughter.

Murray's wife, Katherine Bruce of Clackmannan, had remained at Ham throughout the Civil War, taking charge of their four daughters: Elizabeth, Katherine, Anne and Margaret. Heavy Parliamentary taxes and fines were levied on the estate, but threats of sequestration were skilfully avoided. The house and park were transferred to Katherine's name, and several of her Scots Presbyterian relatives, headed by the powerful Earl of Elgin, were appointed as trustees. 'Mistress Murray' never dared to use the title conferred on her husband by the King, and died at Ham in 1649, leaving her property to be equally divided among the four children. This decision may have been prompted by the physical disabilities of the younger daughters; family tradition maintains that Katherine, Anne and Margaret were hunchbacks, and this is confirmed by a contemporary, Thomas Knyvet, who wrote in 1644 that 'the other three sisters are pitifull crooked things'.

The couple's eldest daughter, Elizabeth, had married Sir Lionel Tollemache in 1648. Tollemache was a wealthy Suffolk landowner of ancient lineage, with impressive seats at Helmingham Hall in Suffolk and Harrington Hall in Northamptonshire. In 1649 he appears to have taken over the administration of Ham on behalf of the four sisters, carefully dividing rental income, and staving off further threats of sequestration.

Lady Tollemache (or Lady Dysart, as she became known after the death of her father) was a young woman of charm and character with flame red hair. Knyvet described her in 1644 as a 'pretty witty lass'. Bishop Burnet (later a critic) conceded:

Elizabeth, Countess of Dysart, with her first husband, Sir Lionel Tollemache, and her sister, Lady Maynard (sitting); attributed to Joan Carlile (Back Parlour)

She was a woman of great beauty, but of far greater parts. She had a wonderfull quickness of apprehension, and an amazing vivacity in conversation. She had studied not only divinity and history, but mathematics and philosophy. She was violent in everything she set about, a violent friend, but a still more violent enemy.

During the Interregnum Elizabeth skilfully played both sides. On the one hand, she established good relations with the Protector: Burnet records, 'Cromwell was certainly fond of her, and she took care to entertain him in it, till he, finding what was said apon it, broke it off'. On the other, she risked imprisonment as a loyal member of the 'Sealed Knot', a secret society that worked for Charles II's restoration. Elizabeth joined her brother-in-law, Sir William Compton, and her father's great friend, Colonel John Russell, in sending coded letters to the Court in exile; the King was known as 'Mr Sloane', Compton was 'Lawton', while Elizabeth herself was 'Mrs Legge'.

While Dames Katherine, Anne and Margaret Murray lived permanently at Ham, Elizabeth and Sir Lionel spent much of the year at Helmingham Hall and their London house in Covent Garden. The young couple do, however, appear to have bought some new furniture for Ham during this period, and were enthusiastic patrons of the painter Peter Lely. The old nursery at Ham (now the Duchess's Bedchamber) was much in use: Elizabeth gave birth to eleven children between 1648 and 1661, five of whom survived to adulthood.

When Charles II was restored to the throne in 1660, Sir Lionel was granted the Rangership of Richmond Park, and Elizabeth was rewarded for her loyalty with a sizeable pension: 'Eight hundred pounds by the yeare to be paid to her out of the receit of the Exchequer during her life'. While she had been somewhat wary of using the title inherited from her father during the Commonwealth, Elizabeth was now universally known as Countess of Dysart in her own right, with her eldest son acknowledged as Viscount Huntingtower.

While Lady Dysart became a prominent figure at the Restoration Court, Sir Lionel increasingly found himself afflicted by ill-health. In the late 1660s he made several trips to France to consult eminent doctors, dying in Paris on 18 January 1669.

CHAPTER FOUR

THE DUKE AND DUCHESS OF LAUDERDALE

Court gossip had for many years linked Lady Dysart's name with that of another Scot, John Maitland, 2nd Earl of Lauderdale. In the early 1650s Elizabeth is said to have used her influence with Cromwell to save Lauderdale's life while he was imprisoned in the Tower. Their friendship rekindled after the Restoration, and became particularly close after the death of Sir Lionel Tollemache in 1669. Lauderdale's wife died in December 1671, and the couple were married early the following year. As Sir George Mackenzie put it:

Lady Dysart had such an ascendant over his affections that neither her age, nor his affairs, nor yet the clamour of his friends, and the people, more urgent than both of these, could divert him from marrying her within six weeks of his Lady's decease.

Judging by his portraits, Lauderdale was not a prepossessing man, but he was able, energetic and intelligent. Bishop Burnet, who knew him well, described his as someone who:

made but an ill appearance, his hair red, his tongue too big for his mouth, and his whole manner rough and boisterous, and very unfit for Court. His temper was intolerable, for he was haughty beyond all expression to all who had expectances from him, but abject where himself had any; and so violently passionate that he often-times, upon slight occasions, ran himself into fits like madness. His learning was considerable, for he not only understood Latin, in which he was a master, but Greek and Hebrew; had read a great deal of divinity, almost all historians both ancient and modern; and having besides an extraordinary memory was furnished with a copious but very unpolished way of expression.

The Earl of Ailesbury noted that Lauderdale was for ever 'uttering bald jests for wit, and repeating good ones for others, and ever spoiled them in relating them, which delighted the good King much'. Less appealingly, 'Lauderdale was continually putting his fingers into the King's snuff box, which obliged him to order one to be made which he wore with a string on his wrist, and did not open, but the snuff came out by shaking.'

Charles II appreciated Lauderdale's ruthless temper, and was amused by his coarseness of manner. Furthermore, his loyalty had been tested to the limit: Lauderdale had been captured by the Parliamentarians at the Battle of Worcester in 1651, and was held prisoner for nine years. In 1661 Charles II appointed Lauderdale Secretary of State for Scotland, in which post he assumed almost vice-regal powers. With no other ministers responsible for Scotland, and provided that he followed the King's policies, he was allowed a free rein to run the country as he pleased. According to Burnet:

The sense of religion that a long imprisonment had impressed on his mind was soon erased by a course of luxury and sensuality, which ran him into a great expense, and which he stuck at nothing to support; and the fury of his behaviour heightened the severity of his ministry, and made it more like the cruelty of an Inquisition than the legality of justice.

Lauderdale also became a key member of the 'Cabal' Ministry – Clifford, Ashley, Buckingham, Arlington and Lauderdale – who formed an inner Cabinet behind which Charles governed in the late 1660s and early 1670s.

Lauderdale was at the height of his power when he married Elizabeth Dysart in 1672. In May that year he received a dukedom, and the couple embarked on a flurry of building to celebrate their new position. In Scotland the Duke asked Elizabeth's cousin, Sir William Bruce, to draw up plans for the remodelling of the Maitland castles of Thirlestane, Lethington and Brunstane; with the King's blessing, drawings were also prepared for the extension of Holyrood Palace. In England, the couple decided to

The Duke and Duchess of Lauderdale at the height of their power; by Peter Lely (Hall Gallery)

refurbish their lodgings in Whitehall Palace, and to double the size of Ham House.

Elizabeth had apparently begun to think of modernising and extending Ham in 1671. Encouraged by Lauderdale (who stayed openly at Ham before his wife's death), she asked Bruce to provide designs for an impressive new entrance gateway. Soon afterwards plans and elevations were prepared for the main item on the building programme: the doubling of the accommodation at Ham by building new rooms along the south front between the two projecting wings. The surviving drawings are attributed to John Slezer, a German engineer and surveyor also employed by Lauderdale at Thirlestane and Lethington. But they were probably produced under the instruction of William Samwell, the English gentleman-architect who actually oversaw the building work. In 1668–71 Samwell had designed Charles II's house at Newmarket, which the Lauderdales would have known well.

Construction of the new south front began early in 1672, and was completed in the summer of 1674. The painting attributed to Henry Danckerts in the White Closet shows the finished exterior, with its sash-windows (a recent invention) cunningly designed with false mullions and transoms to blend with the surviving Jacobean windows. Inside, the new

The Queen's Closet, the most private of the Lauderdales' new State Apartments

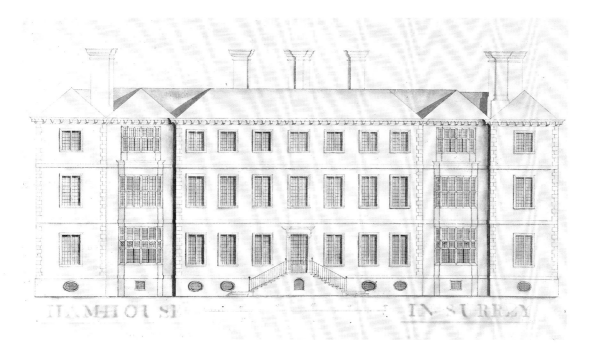

This may be an architect's design for the new south front built in 1672–4 for the Lauderdales

rooms were laid out in a strictly axial plan: on the ground floor, twin sets of rooms for the Duke and Duchess flanked the central Marble Dining Room, while an additional series of State Apartments for the use of Queen Catherine of Braganza filled the floor above. The alterations received high praise from John Evelyn and the architect Roger North, who stated in his *Essay on Building*:

This hous is, in its time, esteemed as one of the beautyful and compleat seats in the kingdome. And all ariseth out of the skill and dexterity in managing the alterations, which in my opinion are the best I have seen. Ffor I doe not perceiv any part of the old fabrick is taken downe, but the wings stand as they were first sett, onely behind, next the garden, they are joyned with a strait rang intirely new. And there are all the rooms of parade, exquisitely plact, and taking in the wings as addittions. . . . so that the visto is compleat from end to end, with a noble roome of entry in the midle, which is used as a dining room.

With the rebuilding complete, decoration of the interior could begin. Fortunately the Duchess kept meticulous accounts during this period, so we know the names of nearly all the craftsmen involved. Joinery and parquetry floors were supplied by Henry Harlow, while more delicate carving was produced by John Bullimore; Henry Wells created the moulded plaster ceilings, and Nicholas Moore did the paintwork and gilding. Foreign craftsmen were also employed: regular payments were made to two Dutch joiners, Henry Mommers and Johan Ulrich, while a Roman, Baldassare Artima, made the impressive scagliola fireplace surround in the Queen's Closet.

The Duke and Duchess also commissioned a series of paintings for ceilings and insets in the panelling, which were conceived as part of the general decorative scheme. Two of the artists involved had already worked for Charles II: the Italian Antonio Verrio, who painted (or directed the painting) of most of the ceilings, and the Dutchman William van de Velde the Younger, who produced the marine overdoors for the Duchess's Bed-chamber (then being used by the Duke). Four further Dutch artists painted inset pictures for Ham: Abraham Begeyn, Dirck van den Bergen, and Thomas and Jan Wyck. A smaller number were supplied by the Scottish painter William Gouw Ferguson.

Sumptuous decoration was followed up by extravagant purchases of furniture and upholstery. John Evelyn, visiting Ham in 1678, described the house as 'furnished like a Great Prince's'. This impression is confirmed by the detailed inventories drawn up in 1677, 1679 and 1683, and by the quality of the contents from that period that still remain. The Duke and Duchess replaced almost every item of William Murray's furnishings. Some pieces were imported from the Continent: regular deliveries from Holland were collected from the London Custom House, and bills survive for mirrors, pier-tables and candlestands bought in Paris from makers such as Antoine Pelletier. The couple also patronised foreign craftsmen resident in England, one of whom was Jean Poitevin; the Duchess favoured French upholsterers and embroiderers, and employed the Low Countries cabinetmaker Gerrit Jensen. Huge sums were spent on textiles and trimmings: in September and October 1673, the Duchess bought a total of 152 tassels made out of gold and silver thread.

This vast rate of expenditure could not go on for ever. In Scotland, Lauderdale's policy had become increasingly severe, and ruthless methods were employed against the Presbyterian adherents of the Covenants, which had been outlawed in 1662. With unpopularity came rumours of corruption and embezzlement; contemporaries also resented the influence of the Duchess, whose greed and hauteur had alienated Scottish courtiers. Bishop Burnet wrote that:

The Lady Dysart came to have so much power over the Lord Lauderdale, that it lessened him much in the esteem of all the world; for he delivered himself up to all her humours and passions. All applications were made to her; she took upon her to determine every thing; she sold all places, and was wanting in no methods that could bring her money, which she lavished out in a most profuse vanity. As the conceit took her, she made him fall out with all his friends, one after another.

Popular lampoons portrayed 'Lidington' (Lauderdale) and 'Hatton' (Lauderdale's brother, Lord Halton) as puppets of the rapacious Lady Dysart:

Methinks this poor land has been troubled too long
With Hatton and Dysart and old Lidington,
These fools who at once make us love and despair
And preclude all the ways to his Majesty's ear.
While justice provokes me in rhyme to expresse,
The truth which I know of my bonnie old Besse.

She is Besse of my heart, she was Besse of old Noll
    [Cromwell];
She was once Fleetwood's [Cromwell's son-in-law]
    Besse, now she's Besse of Atholle [the Earl of
    Atholl];
She's Besse of the Church and Besse of the State,
She plots with her tail, and her lord with his pate.
With a head on one side, and a hand lifted hie,
She kills us with frowning and makes us to die.

Despite Scottish protests, Charles II continued to support Lauderdale until ill-health forced him to resign as Secretary of State in October 1680. Once out of office, however, Lauderdale's influence declined swiftly: by 1682 he had been deprived of most of his positions, and of all pensions to himself and his duchess. The Duke died in August 1682 at Tunbridge Wells, where he had been taking the waters, and was buried in great state in Scotland in April 1683.

To the fury of the Maitland family, Lauderdale

Detail of the blue damask embroidered hangings, which were put up between 1679 and 1683 in the Queen's Antechamber

was found to have left the majority of his Scottish estates, and all his property in England, to his wife. A portrait of the Duke at Thirlestane Castle bears the inscription:

This man enjoy'd all the great offices under the Crown, but ruin'd his family by giving away to an old woman, Lady Dysart, his second wife, an immense Estate handed him through a series of prudent and able ancestors, which estate was the means of raising him to the Honours he enjoy'd.

The Duke's brother and successor as 3rd Earl of Lauderdale was further enraged when the unrepentant Duchess attempted to sue him for the payment of Lauderdale's funeral expenses, which came to the enormous sum of £5,000.

The Duchess's reputation for 'ravenous covetousness' was firmly established during this period. To be fair to her, the couple's building and redecoration programmes in England and Scotland had run up debts so large that they could not even be covered by the sale of property left to her by the Duke. She was forced to take out large mortgages on the Ham estate, and on the house itself. Jewellery, silver and even pictures were pawned for ready money. Jan Wyck was asked to draw up a list of valuations, and many of the smaller pictures still bear an inscription on the rear stating the price for which they could be redeemed. All this does not, however, excuse her behaviour towards the Duke's family: casting desperately about for a solution to her money worries, Elizabeth claimed that the 3rd Earl should be responsible for the Duke's debts in England. When the Earl replied that these debts had been caused by the extension of Ham House, and by the purchase of the Duddingston estate in Scotland, which had been given to the Duchess, she took him to court. Ten years of costly litigation followed, in which neither side was the winner.

After such a full and brilliant life, Elizabeth's last years must have been lonely. Within four years of her husband's death she had retreated entirely from Court life, and spent nearly all her time at Ham. Her last surviving sister, Lady Maynard, died in 1682, and her two younger sons, whom she adored, were both killed in battle in 1694. Her eldest son, Lord Huntingtower, was engrossed with his large Tollemache estates in Suffolk and Northampton-

The plasterwork ceiling of the Queen's Bedchamber was put up for the Lauderdales, probably by Henry Wells

shire, and her daughters – the Duchess of Argyll and the Countess of Sutherland – lived mostly in Scotland. Elizabeth herself suffered increasingly from crippling gout, and her later letters to her children are full of pathos; in 1694 she wrote to the Duchess of Argyll:

It is now more than 8 years since I have been so constantly fixed in this place [Ham House] that I am even a stranger to all others. . . . I have never yet been farther than this lowe story, except when I was had up to the highest to close old Rebecca's eyes. . . . I have now lost my two only youngest sonnes, and all my movable estate is sould (even to the disfurnishing of this my dwelling house). . . . And now what can I or what must I further do? But condemn my own mistaken measurs which have proved so fatal that should I be cutt in pieces to gratify owr Enemyes none of my children nor their children would be the better.

Elizabeth Murray, Countess of Dysart and Duchess of Lauderdale died 'in this lowe story' at Ham House on Sunday, 15 June 1698. In accordance with her wishes, she was buried very quietly, 'carried only by my particular family, in Petersham church where my most honoured mother the Countess of Dysart does lye with three of my sisters and three of my own children'.

CHAPTER FIVE

AFTER 1698

Lionel Tollemache, 3rd Earl of Dysart, inherited Ham House and the Dysart title on the death of his mother in 1698. The inheritance must initially have seemed more of a burden than a blessing: the Duchess's financial affairs remained in turmoil, and the house had received few repairs since the early 1680s. Lionel and his wife, Grace Wilbraham, were in any case well established elsewhere. The 3rd Earl already owned three substantial seats, each with large estates: Helmingham and Harrington, and Woodhey in Cheshire.

The 3rd Earl cannot perhaps be blamed for taking little interest in a house that had been so much his mother's creation. No structural repairs appear to

Lionel, 3rd Earl of Dysart; by David Paton

have been made during this period, although an inventory made in 1728 shows that he and his wife did make some internal changes. Most notable of these was the piercing of the floor dividing the old Great Dining Room from the Great Hall to make the present Hall Gallery. The Earl, who had created an elaborate Italianate terraced garden at Harrington in the 1670s, also ensured that the garden was well maintained. Surviving accounts for Ham record regular payments to gardeners, and Macky's 1724 *Journey into England* noted that while the house was 'more neglected than one would expect for so great an estate . . . the gardens are well kept up'.

Unlike his mother, the 3rd Earl was always extremely careful (perhaps too careful) with money. Humphrey Prideaux wrote in 1696, 'The frugal and sparing way of living which his circumstances at first made necessary hath habituated him to that which, now he is out of those circumstances, is downright stinginess'. This 'stinginess' was particularly evident in his treatment of his eldest son, Lord Huntingtower, who made a runaway marriage with Henrietta Cavendish, illegitimate daughter of the 2nd Duke of Devonshire. Lord Dysart disapproved of the match, and initially refused to finance the young couple. Mrs Manley wrote in her memoirs:

Lord Dysart's parsimonious irreconcilable Temper has made him forget that this young Lord is his child, and that the young Gentleman can't but desire the Death of his Father, that Himself, his Wife, and Little ones may have enough to eat. . . . Relent, Relent, un-natural Father, before it is too late.

Lord Dysart must have relented, for his grandson and eventual heir, Lionel, was born at Helmingham Hall in 1708. Young Lionel became the 4th Earl of Dysart on his grandfather's death in 1727, and soon afterwards embarked on a Grand Tour of France, Switzerland and Italy. He returned in 1728, and married in the following year Lady Grace Carteret, daughter of John, 2nd Baron Carteret and later 2nd Earl Granville. Grace was a talented amateur artist, who painted pastel portraits of her family, and decorated furniture with intricate shellwork. She also loved richly coloured dresses and textiles; her cousin, the diarist Mrs Delany, often praised her clothes. At a Court Ball in 1739, 'Lady Dysart was in a scarlet damask gown, facings and robings embroidered with gold and colours, her petticoat white satin, all covered with embroidery of the same sort, very fine and handsome'. Mrs Delany was less complimentary regarding her character. In the same passage she notes, 'But her gaiety was all external, for at heart she is the most wretched virtuous woman that I know'.

Soon after their marriage, the young couple embarked on a series of improvements at their two main seats, Helmingham and Ham. At Ham the 4th Earl commissioned a detailed structural survey from the architect John James. The exterior of the house was found to be in a very poor condition; James recorded in June 1730 that the bay windows were 'entirely ruinous and incapable of Repair otherwise than by Re-building them', while the frontispiece over the front door was 'drawn off from the Wall, from the bottom to the top . . . it has gone so far as to endanger even pulling the Roof after it'. The 4th Earl's account books show that repairs continued through the 1740s and '50s, during which time the bays on the north and south fronts were completely rebuilt, the frontispiece removed, the roofline straightened, and all the sash-windows replaced.

Inside the house, the 4th Earl made many fashionable alterations. On the ground floor, the Great Hall was refurnished, the Marble Dining Room redecorated, and a new family drawing-room created from the old Volury Room. On the first floor, the Queen's Bedchamber was transformed into a formal drawing-room, and on the second floor bedrooms were wallpapered and brought up to date. The 4th Earl filled the rooms at Ham with the latest furniture and upholstery. Thanks to his meticulous bookkeeping system, many of the accounts and bills for these purchases survive: from William Bradshaw the 4th Earl bought gilded mirrors, pier-tables and tapestries after Watteau and

Lionel, 4th Earl of Dysart; by Rosalba Carriera (collection Lord Tollemache)

Pater; from Henry Heasman the latest silk damasks, festoon curtains and canopied beds; from George Nix and John Hele mahogany chairs and tables; from John Sutton embossed leather wall-hangings. A regular auction-goer, Lord Dysart also established an impressive library, and bought new paintings and reframed others.

The 4th Earl died in 1770, and was succeeded by his eldest son, another Lionel. Relations between father and son had become strained after Lord Huntingtower's secret marriage to Charlotte Walpole in 1760. Charlotte was the youngest of the illegitimate daughters of Sir Edward Walpole, and niece of Horace Walpole, who lived across the river from Ham at Strawberry Hill. Walpole wrote to George Conway describing the awkward situation:

I announce my Lady Huntingtower to you. I hope you will approve the match a little more than I suppose my Lord Dysart will, as he does not know yet, though they have been married these two hours, that at ten o'clock this morning his son espous'd my niece Charlotte at St James' Church.

Louisa, 7th Countess of Dysart; by John Hoppner after
Sir Joshua Reynolds (Great Hall)

For Charlotte, the union was a practical rather than a romantic one; according to Walpole, she told her sister that:

If I was but nineteen I would refuse point blank. I do not like to be married in a week to a man I never saw. But I am two-and-twenty. Some people say I am handsome, some say I am not. I believe the truth is that I am likely to be large and go off soon. It is dangerous to refuse so great a match.

Charlotte was not in fact to receive the full benefits of her choice for ten years; Lord Dysart refused to make any settlement on the young couple, and allowed his son an allowance of only £400 a year.

The 5th Earl and his bride finally took possession

of their inheritance in 1770. Walpole immediately seized the opportunity to look round Ham House:

I went yesterday to see my niece in her new principality of Ham. It delighted me and made me peevish. Close to the Thames in the centre of all rich and verdant beauty, it is so blocked up and barricaded with walls, vast trees, and gates, that you think of yourself an hundred miles off and an hundred years back. The old furniture is so magnificently ancient, dreary and decayed, that at every step one's spirits sink, and all my passion for antiquity could not keep them up. Every minute I expected to see ghosts sweeping by; ghosts I would not give sixpence to see, Lauderdales, Tallemachs and Maitlands. There is an old brown gallery full of Vandycks and Lelys, charming miniatures, delightful Wouvermans, and Polenburghs, china, japan, bronzes, ivory cabinets, and silver dogs, pokers, bellows etc, without end. One pair of bellows is of filigree. In this state of pomp and tatters my nephew intends it shall remain, and is so religious an observer of the venerable rites of his house, that because the gates were never opened by his father but once for the late Lord Granville, you are locked out and locked in, and after journeying all round the house as you do round an old French fortified town, you are at last admitted through the stableyard to creep along a dark passage by the house-keepers room, and so by a back door to the Great Hall.

Unfortunately for Charlotte, the 5th Earl appears to have become increasingly miserly and reclusive as he grew older. It was during this period that the two subsidiary Tollemache seats, Harrington Hall and Woodhey, were demolished, and there appears to have been little money spent on maintenance at Helmingham or Ham. Visitors to Ham were often turned away. When George III, curious to see the old house with its many relics of an earlier age, invited himself over from Windsor, his messenger returned with the reply from Lord Dysart that 'Whenever my house becomes a public spectacle, His Majesty shall certainly have the first view'.

In 1799 the 5th Earl died childless, and was succeeded by his brother, Wilbraham, as 6th Earl. Wilbraham was a cultured and sociable man, who had pursued a successful independent career – first as

(Opposite) The Great Hall; watercolour by
H. W. Brewer, 1886 (private collection)

a Member of Parliament, and latterly as High Sheriff of Cheshire. As the writer of the family history, Major-General Edward Tollemache, put it:

Wilbraham, sixth Earl of Dysart, was as desirable a head of the family as his elder brother had been unworthy. He had a profound knowledge of the world and of county conditions, and took a great interest in the management of his estates. He was cultivated and accomplished, and had inherited his mother's talent for painting. During his life open hospitality was kept up at Ham House.

Ham appears to have undergone something of a renaissance during this period. Queen Charlotte, writing in 1809, noted:

The house is much altered since I saw it by repairing, and tho' the old furniture still remains, it is now kept so clean, that even under the tattered state of hangings and chairs, one must admire the good taste of our forefathers and their magnificence. The parquet floors have been taken up with great care, cleaned and relaid, and in order to preserve them the present lord has put carpets over them, but, of course, not nailed down.

Interest in old buildings and their furnishings was becoming more widespread in the early nineteenth century, and the 6th Earl appears to have approached redecoration at Ham in an antiquarian spirit, most notably in his treatment of the Great Staircase. He commissioned exact replicas of seventeenth-century chairs already in the house, and appears to have filled out gaps in the picture-hang with appropriately framed seventeenth-century pictures from Helmingham. New materials were cleverly mingled with old: in the new Yellow Satin Bedroom, the walls were hung with modern striped silk, but the new mahogany bedstead was upholstered with eighteenth-century embroidered satin bought a generation before. Queen Charlotte concluded, 'Upon the whole, the place remaining in its old style is beautiful and magnificent both within and without, but truly melancholy'.

The 6th Earl died childless in 1821, and the Tollemache estates were divided between his surviving sister, Lady Louisa Manners, and the children of his deceased sister, Lady Jane Halliday. At the age of 76, Lady Louisa became Countess of Dysart in her own right, inheriting Ham House and its surrounding lands in perpetuity, and Helmingham Hall for life.

Lady Jane's eldest son, Admiral John Delap Halliday, changed his name to Tollemache and inherited the extensive estates in Suffolk, Northamptonshire and Cheshire. The elderly Countess appears to have been an efficient administrator, but made few changes at either Helmingham or Ham. The 1844 Ham inventory taken four years after her death accordingly reflects the rearrangements made by her father and brother, the 4th and 6th Earls. She was, however, an early patron of Constable, who drew in the park at Helmingham in 1800. Constable copies of Tollemache portraits are in store at Ham today.

On Lady Louisa's death in 1840, Helmingham passed to her nephew, the Admiral, father of the 1st Lord Tollemache, and Ham to her grandson, Lionel, 8th Earl of Dysart. Lord Dysart also inherited Buckminster Park, Grantham, and estates in Leicestershire – the property of Lady Louisa's husband, John Manners. The 8th Earl, like the 5th, soon gained the reputation of a miser and a recluse. Lord Dysart spent little time at Ham, preferring his London house in Norfolk Street; family tradition maintains that he seldom went outside, retreating into a single room, into which food was passed through a trap door.

While the 8th Earl lurked in Norfolk Street, his eldest son, William, Lord Huntingtower, made somewhat scandalous use of Ham. Lord Huntingtower was a notorious rake, who openly ran several households, resulting in an embarrassing legitimacy case in 1881. A leader in *The Times* from that year records:

Repudiated by his parents, in constant strife with the cousin he had persuaded to marry him as a reformed rake, sued in the County Courts and by parish guardians, chained to an illiterate woman he had seduced . . . he had done all in his power before he was thirty to wreck the noble inheritance of his ancestors.

Lord Huntingtower lived at Ham until his death in 1872 at the age of 52. A group of cousins, headed by the brothers Algernon and Frederick Tollemache, then moved into the house to act as guardians and administrators for Lord Huntingtower's thirteen-year-old son, William John. It was during this period of confusion and neglect that Augustus Hare visited Ham, and recorded that:

No half-inhabited chateau of a ruined family in Normandy was ever so dilapidated as this home of the enormously rich Tollemaches. Like a French chateau too is the entrance through a gateway to a desolate yard with old trees and a sundial, and a donkey feeding. All the members of the family whom I knew were absent, but I sent in my card to Mr Algernon Tollemache, who received us. As the door at the head of the entrance-stair opened, its handle went through a priceless Sir Joshua of Louisa, Countess of Dysart; it always does go through it. We were taken through a half-ruined hall and a bedroom to an inner room [the Duchess's Bedchamber] in which Mr Algernon Tollemache (unable to move from illness) was sitting. It presented the most unusual contrasts imaginable – a velvet bed in a recess backed by the most exquisite embroidery on Chinese silk; an uncarpeted floor of rough boards; a glorious Lely portrait of the Duchess of Lauderdale; a deal board by way of a washing stand, with a coarse white jug and basin upon it; a splendid mirror framed in massive silver on a hideous rough deal scullery table without a cover; and all Mr Tollemache's most extraordinary huge boots and shoes ranged around the room by way of ornament.

William John succeeded his grandfather as 9th Earl of Dysart in 1878, but did not gain full control of the estate until his 25th birthday in 1884. An inventory taken in that year, and a series of watercolours painted in 1886, record the house before Lord Dysart began a comprehensive programme of repair and restoration. Structural and practical works were tackled first: the arcades on the north front were completely rebuilt, and iron girders inserted in the roof; central heating and electric lighting installed throughout the house, and crumbling deal floorboards replaced by modern parquet. The 9th Earl then moved on to furnishing and decoration: between 1892 and 1893 a team of in-house restorers repaired 136 individual items of furniture. Decaying silk hangings, curtains and upholstery were replaced in many rooms, with care often taken to replicate the original colours and patterns, as in the Green Closet. Lord Dysart also provided every bedroom in the house with a new brass bed, and repainted the Great Hall in a striking scheme of deep green and gold.

(Right) The 9th Earl; by Alexander Macdonald, 1879

The state of Ham House at the turn of the century – its rooms filled with a plethora of furniture, arranged in cluttered Victorian style – is enshrined in Julia Roundell's *Ham House, its History and Art Treasures* (1904). Ham's 'Sleeping Beauty' quality then became renowned; the house was described by Avray Tipping in his *English Homes* (1920), and illustrated articles appeared in *Country Life* and elsewhere. The 9th Earl died childless in 1935, when the title passed to his niece Wynefrede. Ham was entailed on his male heirs, however, as was the usual English custom, and thus passed to his second cousin Sir Lyonel Tollemache, 4th Bt. In March 1943 James Lees-Milne, the National Trust's first Historic Buildings Secretary, visited the house to discuss its future:

The grounds are indescribably overgrown and unkempt. I passed long ranges of semi-derelict outhouses. The garden is pitted with bomb craters around the house, from which a few windows have been blown

out and the busts from the niches torn away. . . . Sir Lyonel was sitting in an upright chair. He was dressed . . . immaculately in a grey suit, beautifully pressed, and wore a stock tie with large pearl pin. I think he had spats over black polished shoes. A very decorative figure, and very courteous. . . . There is no doubt whatever that even without the contents this house is worthy of acceptance because of the superlative interior treatment, the panelling, the exquisite parquetry floors, the extraordinary chimneypieces, the great staircase of pierced balusters, the velvet hangings.

Sir Lyonel and his son, Cecil Tollemache, generously presented Ham to the National Trust in 1948. The Trust in turn leased the house to the Ministry of Works. The contents were purchased by the Government and entrusted to the care of the Victoria & Albert Museum, which administered the house for many years. On the basis of archival research, the museum embarked around 1970 upon a pioneering rearrangement and redecoration of the interior along seventeenth century lines. In 1990 the Government relinquished its lease of Ham, and the Victoria & Albert Museum generously placed the contents on long loan to the National Trust. Compensation for the unexpired portion of the lease has been used to form a quasi-endowment.

Since 1990, the Trust has undertaken extensive repairs with the principal aim of improving the services. It hopes to continue the museum's policy of commissioning authentic copies of fabrics described in the seventeenth-century and subsequent accounts. The pictures have been newly arranged following the inventories, and the Entrance Hall and Great Staircase redecorated. Future plans include the re-creation of the 4th Earl's 1740s drawing-room in the Volury Room, and the restoration of the 6th Earl's Yellow Satin Bedroom as decorated in 1813.

The Yellow Satin Bedroom in 1920

FAMILY TREE

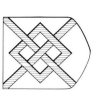

WILLIAM MURRAY, 1ST EARL OF DYSART* = KATHERINE BRUCE* (d.1649) of Clackmannan
(c.1600–55)

ELIZABETH MURRAY = (1) Sir Lionel Tollemache, 3rd Bt*
COUNTESS OF DYSART later COUNTESS   (1624–69)
and DUCHESS OF LAUDERDALE*   (2) John Maitland, 2nd Earl and 1st Duke
(1626–98)   of Lauderdale* (1616–1682)

KATHERINE* (d.1669/70)

ANNE (d.1679)

MARGARET LADY MAYNARD* (c.1638–82)

LIONEL TOLLEMACHE = Grace Wilbraham*
3rd EARL OF DYSART* (d.1740)
(1649–1727)

Gen. Thomas* (c.1651–94)

Capt. William (d.1694)

Elizabeth, Lady Lorne, later Duchess of Argyll* (1659–1735)

Katherine, Viscountess Doune, later Countess of Sutherland (1661–1703)

Lionel Tollemache = Henrietta Cavendish*
Viscount Huntingtower (1682–1712)   (d.1717/18)

LIONEL TOLLEMACHE = Lady Grace Carteret*
4th EARL OF DYSART* (1708–70)   (1713–55)

LIONEL TOLLEMACHE   Frances*   WILBRAHAM = Anna Maria   John* = Lady   Louisa = John   Jane = (1) John Halliday
5th EARL OF DYSART*   (1738–   TOLLEMACHE   Lewis   (1744–77) Bridget   COUNTESS OF Manners   (1750–   (2) George Ferry
(1734–99)   1807)   6th EARL OF (1745–1804)   Lane   LYSART*   (1730–92) 1802)
                                        DYSART*   Fox   (1745–1840)
                                        (1739–1821)

LIONEL = (1) Charlotte Walpole*   Lionel Robert* (1779–93)   Admiral John (Halliday) Tollemache = Lady Elizabeth Stratford
TOLLEMACHE   (1738–89)   cr. Bt 1793, assumed name and arms of Tollemache 1821   (1772–1837)   (d.1861)
(1734–99) (2) Magdalena Lewis
           (d.1823)

Sir William Tollemache, Viscount Huntingtower (1766–1833) = Catherine Gray   John, cr. Baron Tollemache = Georgina Best
          (1766–1852)   of Helmingham   (1805–90)
                               (d.1846)

LIONEL TOLLEMACHE = Elizabeth Toone   Felix = Sarah Gray   Hugh = Matilda Hume   Wilbraham = (1) Lady Emma Stuart (d.1869)   Hamilton = Mabel Hanbury
8th EARL OF DYSART   (d.1869)   (1796–1843) (d.1831)   (1802–90) (d.1873)   2nd Baron Tollemache   (2) Hon. Mary Hamilton   (1852–93) (d.1941)
(1794–1878)   (1832–1904)   (d.1939)

William Tollemache = Katherine Burke   Caroline   Ralph = Caroline Tollemache   Hon. Lyonel = Lady Blanche King   Edward = Violet Ridgeway
Viscount Huntingtower   (1822–96)   (d.1867)   (1826–95) (1828–67)   (1860–1902)   (d.1953)   (1885–   (d.1970)
(1820–72)   Sir LYONEL = Hersilia Collingwood   1947)

WILLIAM TOLLEMACHE = Cecilia Onslow Newton   Agnes = Charles Scott   TOLLEMACHE, 4th Bt = Hersilia Collingwood   John, 4th Baron = Dinah Jamieson
9th EARL OF DYSART*   (d.1917)   (1853–1912) (1853–1938)   (1854–1952)   Tollemache (1910–75)
(1859–1935)

Wynefrede = Owain Greaves   Sir CECIL LYONEL   Sir Humphry = Nora Taylor   Bentley = Wynford Kemball   Timothy, 5th Baron Tollemache = Alexandra Meynell
Countess of Dysart   m.1913   TOLLEMACHE, 5th Bt   6th Bt   m.1926   3rd Baron Tollemache   (d.1926)   (b.1939)
(1889–1973)   (1882–1941)   (1886–1969)   (1897–1990)   (1883–1955;
                                        gave Ham to NT 1948

Rosamund, Countess   Katherine = John Peter Grant of Rothiemurchus
of Dysart (b.1914)   (b.1918) m.1941 (d.1987)

Sir Lyonel, 7th Bt = Mary Whitbread
(b.1931)   m.1960

CONFIDO CONQUIESCO
I trust and am content

Owners of Ham
are shown in CAPITALS

Asterisk denotes a portrait
in the house

BIBLIOGRAPHY

MANUSCRIPT SOURCES

The Tollemache Papers are in the Buckminster Estate Office, Grantham, Lincolnshire, at Helmingham Hall, Suffolk, and in Kingston Record Office, Kingston, Surrey.

PUBLISHED SOURCES

BROWN, Jane, *The Art and Architecture of English Gardens*, 1989, pp. 32–3.

CORNFORTH, John, 'Ham House Re-interpreted', *Country Life*, clxix, 29 January and 5 February 1981, pp.250, 322.

CRIPPS, Doreen, *Elizabeth of the Sealed Knot*, 1975.

DAVIDSON, Caroline, *The Ham House Kitchen*, n.d.

DUNBAR, J., 'The Building Activities of the Duke and Duchess of Lauderdale, 1670–82', *Archaeological Journal*, cxxxii, 1975.

FISHER, J., *Mr Marshall's Flower Album from the Royal Library at Windsor Castle*, 1985.

FRASER, Antonia, 'Bess and Old Noll', *Horizon*, Autumn 1971.

GIROUARD, Mark, 'The Smythson Collection', *Architectural History*, v, 1962.

JACKSON-STOPS, Gervase, 'A Thames-side Parterre', *Country Life*, October 1975.

JACKSON-STOPS, Gervase, ed., *The Treasure Houses of Britain*, 1985.

LAING, Alastair, and STRACHEY, Nino, 'The Duke and Duchess of Lauderdale's pictures at Ham House', *Apollo*, May 1994.

ROUNDELL, Julia, *Ham House, its History and Art Treasures*, 1904.

STRONG, Roy, *The Renaissance Garden in England*, 1979.

THORNTON, Peter, and TOMLIN, Maurice, 'The Furnishing and Decoration of Ham House', *Furniture History*, xvi, 1980.

THORNTON, Peter, and TOMLIN, Maurice, 'Franz Cleyn at Ham House', *National Trust Studies*, 1980, pp.21–34.

THORNTON, Peter, 'Magnificence in Miniature – the Ham House Model', *Country Life*, clxiii, 26 January 1978, p.206.

THORNTON, Peter, 'Furniture from the Netherlands at Ham House', *Nederlands Kunshistorisch Jaarboek*, 1980.

TOLLEMACHE, Maj.-Gen. Edward, *The Tollemaches of Helmingham and Ham*, 1949.

TOMLIN, Maurice, 'From Love-Seats to Firescreens – 18th century Furnishings at Ham House', *Country Life*, clxii, 10 November 1977, p.1418.

Verrio's ceiling painting in the White Closet depicts 'Divine Wisdom presiding over the Liberal Arts'

INDEX

Page numbers in *italic* refer to illustrations

Ailesbury, Earl of 64
Artima, Baldassare 67

Begeyn, Abraham 67
Bradshaw, William 71
Brewer, H. W. *15, 19, 22, 26, 33, 73*
Brown, Lancelot 'Capability' 55
Bruce, Katherine, Countess of Dysart (d.1649) *40,* 62–3
Bruce, Sir William 52, 64–5
Brunstane, Edinburgh 64
Buckminster Park, Grantham 74
Bullimore, John 67
Burnet, Bishop Gilbert 61, 63, 64, 68

'Cabal' Ministry 64
Carlile, Joan 63
Carriera, Rosalba *71*
Carter, Thomas 61
Carteret, Lady Grace (later Dysart) (1713–55) 71
Carteret, John, 2nd Earl Granville 71
Catherine of Braganza, Queen 67
Cavendish, Henrietta (later Tollemache) (d. 1717/18) 70
Charles I, King of England 5, *23,* 60–1, *62*
Charles II, King of England 63, 64, 65, 67
Charlotte, Queen Consort 74
Civil War 5, 52
Cleyn, Franz 61
Coade stone *River God 7,* 55
Compton, Sir William 63
Constable, John 74
Conway, George 71
Correggio, Antonio da 61
Country Life 75
Covent Garden, London 63
Cromwell, Oliver 63, 68

Danckerts, Henry *59,* 65
Delany, Mrs 71
Duddingston estate, Edinburgh 69
Dysart, Earls of *see* Tollemache

Dysart, Elizabeth, Countess of *see* Murray
Dysart, Fife 60

English Homes (Tipping) 75
Essay on Building (North) 66
European Architectural Heritage Year (1975) 56
Evelyn, John 52, 67, 68

Ferguson, William Gouw 68

Gainsborough, Thomas 5
George III, King of England 72
Gerbier, Balthazar 61
Goodricke, Matthew 61
Greaves, Wynefrede, Countess of Dysart (1889–1973) 75
Griffin, gardener 55

Halliday, Admiral John Delap (later Tollemache) (1772–1837) 74
Halton, Lord 68
Ham House: building (1610) 5, 52, 60; inventory (1655) 61; inventory (1679) 52, 58; Lauderdales' alterations (1670s) 5, 52, 58, 65–7, *68;* Murray's alterations (1637–9) 5, 52, 61; National Trust acquires (1948) 5, 56, 75–6; repairs (1730s) 5, 71; repairs (1890s) 5, 75; Smythson's plan (1609) 52, 53, *53,* 60
Exterior 6–9, 60: east front *7;* north forecourt *6, 7, 53, 76;* north front *4,* 6–7; south front 7–9, *9, 59, 65, 67;* west side *9*
Interior 9–51: Back Parlour 47–8, *63;* Basement 49–50; Buttery 49; Chapel 12–13, *13;* Duchess's Bathroom 51; Duchess's Bedchamber 45–6, 63, 67; Duchess's Private Closet 41–3, *41, 42;* Duke and Duchess's Apartments 37–46; Duke's Closet 46–7; Duke's Dressing Room *43,* 43–4; Great Dining Room (now Hall Gallery) 5; Great Hall 9–12, *10, 11,* 71, *72, 73, 75,* 76; Great Staircase 5, 13–16, *15,* 61, 74, 76; Green Closet 25–9, *26, 27, 28,*

61, 75; Hall Gallery 5, 9–12, 16–18, 61, 70; Kitchen and Pantry 50–1, *50;* Library 30–1, *31;* Library Closet 29–30; Long Gallery 5, 20–5, *21, 22,* 61; Marble Dining Room 35–7, *36,* 67, 71; Museum Room 16; North Drawing Room 5, 18–20, 61, *62;* Queen's Antechamber 31–3, *32, 68;* Queen's Bedchamber 5, 33–5, *33, 34, 69,* 71; Queen's Closet *1,* 35, *66, 67;* Servants' Hall 51; Steward's Hall 47; Volury Room 39–40, *39,* 71, *76;* West Passage 48–9; White Closet 40–1, 65; Withdrawing Room 37–8; Yellow Satin Bedroom (Lady Maynard's Chamber) 5, 16, 74, 76
Garden 52–9, 70: Cherry Garden 53, 55, 56, *57, 58;* Melancholy Walk 57; North Meadow 56–7; Orangery Garden 55, 59; plans 52–3, *53, 54, 56–7;* South Terrace and Plats 58; West Courtyard and Orchard 59; Wilderness 55, 56, 58
Ham House, its History and Treasures (Roundell) 75
Ham, manor of 61
Hare, Augustus 74–5
Harlow, Henry 67
Harrington Hall, Northants 63, 72
Heasman, Henry 71
Hele, John 71
Helmingham Hall, Suffolk 5, 63, 71
Henri IV, King of France 52
Henrietta Maria, Queen Consort 62
Holland 62
Holyrood Palace, Edinburgh 64
Hoppner, John *72*
Hoskins, John 61

James I, King of England 5, 60
James, John 71
Jensen, Gerrit 68
Jones, Inigo 61
Journal into England (Macky) 70

Kinsman, Joseph 61
Knyvet, Thomas 63

Lauderdale, John, 1st Duke of
    see Maitland
Lauderdale, Elizabeth, Duchess of
    see Murray
Le Sueur, Hubert *40*
Lees-Milne, James 75
'Legge, Mrs' (pseud.) 63
Lely, Sir Peter 63, 75, 65
Lethington Castle 52, 64
Long, George 55

Macdonald, Alexander 75
Mackenzie, Sir George 64
Maitland family 68–9
Maitland, Charles, 3rd Earl of
    Lauderdale (d.1691) 69
Maitland, John, 1st Duke of
    Lauderdale (1616–82) 5, 52, 64–8,
    65
Manley, Mrs 70
Manners, John (1730–92) 74
Manners, Louisa, 7th Countess of
    Dysart (1745–1840) 72, 74, 75
Maynard, Lady Margaret (née
    Murray) (c.1638–82) 62, 63, 69
Mollet, Claude I 52
Mommers, Henry 67
Moore, Nicholas 67
Murray, Anne (d.1679) 62, 63
Murray, Elizabeth, Countess of
    Dysart and Duchess of Lauderdale
    (1626–98) 5, 52, 62, 63, 63, 64–9,
    65, 75
Murray, Katherine (d.1669/70) 62, 63
Murray, Katherine (née Bruce)
    (d.1649), Countess of Dysart *40*,
    62–3
Murray, Margaret (later Maynard)
    (c.1638–82) 62, 63, 69
Murray, Thomas 60
Murray, William, 1st Earl of Dysart
    (c.1600–55) 5, 52, 60, 60–2, 68
Murrays of Tullibardine 60

National Trust, acquires Ham
    House 5, 56, 75–6
Newmarket, Cambs. 65
Nix, George 71
Norfolk Street, London 74
North, Roger 67

Palmere, Roberto 52
Paton, David *61, 70*
Pelletier, Antoine 68
Petersham church 69
Petersham manor 61
Poitevin, Jean 68
Porter, Endymion 61
Prideaux, Humphry 70

Ramsay, John, 1st Earl of
    Holdernesse 60
Reynolds, Sir Joshua 5, *72*, 75
Richmond Borough Council 57
Richmond Park 61
Rocque, John 57
Roundell, Julia 75
Rowlandson, Thomas 55, 56
Russell, Colonel John 63

Samwell, William 65
Scott, Wynefrede, Countess of
    Dysart (later Greaves) (1889–1973)
    75
'Sealed Knot' society 63
Slezer, John 52, 54, 56, 58, 65
Smythson, Robert 52, 53, 53, 60
St-Germain-en-Laye 52
Strawberry Hill, Twickenham 71
Sutton, John 71

Thirlestane Castle, Berwickshire 64,
    69
Thoresby, Ralph 57
Tipping, H. Avray 75
Titian 61
Tollemache, Algernon 74
Tollemache, Sir Cecil Lyonel, 5th Bt
    (1886–1969) 5, 76
Tollemache, Charlotte (née Walpole)
    (1738–89) 71–2
Tollemache, Major-General
    Edward 74
Tollemache, Elizabeth (later Duchess
    of Argyll) (1659–1735) 69
Tollemache, Elizabeth, Countess of
    Dysart and Duchess of Lauderdale
    (1626–98) 5, 52, 62, 63, 63, 64–9,
    65, 75
Tollemache, Frederick 74
Tollemache, Lady Grace (née
    Carteret) (1713–55) 71
Tollemache, Grace (née Wilbraham)
    (d.1740) 70
Tollemache, Henrietta (née
    Cavendish) (d.1717/18) 70
Tollemache, John Delap (Halliday),
    Admiral (1772–1837) 74
Tollemache, Katherine, (later
    Countess of Sutherland) (1661–
    1703) 69
Tollemache, Sir Lionel, 3rd Bt
    (1624–69) 5, 63, 63
Tollemache, Lionel, 3rd Earl of
    Dysart (1649–1727) 5, 55, 69, 70, 70
Tollemache, Lionel, 4th Earl of
    Dysart (1708–70) 5, 53, 55, 70–1, 71
Tollemache, Lionel, 5th Earl of
    Dysart (1734–99) 5, 55, 71–2

Tollemache, Lionel, 8th Earl of Dysart
    (1794–1878) 74
Tollemache, Lionel, Viscount
    Huntingtower (1682–1712) 70
Tollemache, Louisa, 7th Countess of
    Dysart (later Manners) (1745–1840)
    72, 74, 75
Tollemache, Sir Lyonel, 4th Bt
    (1854–1952) 5, 75–6
Tollemache, Wilbraham, 6th Earl of
    Dysart (1739–1821) 5, *17*, 55, 56,
    72–4
Tollemache, William John,
    9th Earl of Dysart (1859–1935)
    5, 74–5, 75
Tollemache, William, Viscount
    Huntingtower (1820–72) 74
Tunbridge Wells, Kent 68

Ulrich, Johan 67

Van de Velde, William the
    Younger 67
Van den Bergen, Dirck 67
Van Dyck, Sir Anthony *23*
Vavasour, Sir Thomas 5, 52, 60
Verrio, Antonio 67
Victoria & Albert Museum,
    London 76
Vitruvius Britannicus (1739) 53–5, 55

Walpole, Charlotte (later Dysart)
    (1738–89) 71–2
Walpole, Sir Edward 71
Walpole, Horace 71, 72
Wells, Henry 67
'Whitehall Group' 61
Whitehall Palace, London 61, 65
Wilbraham, Grace (later Dysart)
    (d.1740) 70
Woodhey 72
Worcester, Battle of (1651) 64
Works, Ministry of 76
Worlidge, John 57
Wright, gardener 55
Wright, Robert 62
Wyck, Jan 52, 54, 56, 58, 67, 69
Wyck, Thomas 67